Advance Praise

"This book is a monumental gift to everyone who is or loves someone living with the fallout from intergenerational trauma. Like the K-drama from which it draws its inspiration, *Daughter of Korean Freud* is full of twists and turns even as it gives an unwavering view of a path toward healing. Hake, who has served as a guiding light for her clients for a long time, has shared the power of self-healing by telling her own story with her unforgettable book."

—**Alison O'Reilly Poage, library director, Seminary of the Southwest**

"A heartbreaking but inspirational journey about overcoming the deep, unjust wounds of a horrific childhood. Heawon Hake's story proves the truth of Nietzsche's adage, 'What doesn't kill you makes you stronger.' Highly recommend!"

—**Suzanne McKenna Link, author of contemporary fiction and romance**

"Heawon Hake's story is written with such raw intensity it touches all of your emotions. Instead of being destroyed by their experiences, Heawon and Woo-ri persisted and thrived. A testament of soul-searching survival and renewal, *Daughter of Korean Freud* is ultimately not about forgiving your abuser, but learning to love yourself."

—**Marjorie Peter, MS Ed, SBL/SDL**

"'He's right to ignore the chaos...' This line grabbed me and pulled me into Heawon Hake's fascinating memoir, *Daughter of Korean Freud*. Hake invites us into Woo-ri's world, which is so unimaginable and confounding, yet she somehow stays afloat through the chaos. Reading this memoir feels like a privilege, as it allows us into a private hell—but also a triumphant journey and incredible emergence into freedom."

—**Robin McKinnon, MS Ed, LCSW**

"This book touched the depths of my soul. Heawon Hake's poignant description of a young girl who feels invisible while suffering unspeakable abuse at the hands of a loved one is balanced by her zest and determination for life and love. The approach to storytelling, through ongoing conversations Hake had with a friend and with a client, brings the richness of the characters to life. An unexpected plot twist at the end is both brilliant and jaw-dropping. An absolute treasure of a book."

—**Karen McMahon, CEO, Journey Beyond Coaching**

Daughter of Korean Freud

Daughter of Korean Freud

HEAWON HAKE

KAP BOOKS · NEW YORK

Daughter of Korean Freud

Copyright 2023, Heawon Hake

All rights reserved. No part of this publication may be reproduced or transmitted in any form or by any means, mechanical or electronic, including photocopying and recording, or by any information storage and retrieval system, without permission in writing from author (except by a reviewer, who may quote brief passages and/or show brief video clips in a review).

Disclaimer: This book is a creative memoir. It reflects the author's present recollections of experiences over time. Some names have been changed or details limited or modified to protect privacy. Other events were omitted, compressed, or fabricated, and dialogue has been recreated.

ISBN: 979-8-218-23107-1 (paperback)
ISBN: 979-8-218-23108-8 (e-book)

Library of Congress Control Number: 2023914650

Edited by Scott and Jocelyn Carbonara, Spiritus Communications
Cover design by Patrick Atkins
Interior design by Jenny Lisk

Published by KAP Books, South Setauket, New York, USA

I would like to dedicate this book to all my past, present, and future clients. They are my teachers and inspirations. They are the reason for what I do. Thank you!

Contents

Foreword Jennifer Gimenez	xi
Introduction	1
Chapter 1	3
Chapter 2	9
Chapter 3	21
Chapter 4	31
Chapter 5	41
Chapter 6	49
Chapter 7	59
Chapter 8	73
Chapter 9	89
Chapter 10	99
Chapter 11	111
Chapter 12	123
Chapter 13	135
Chapter 14	143
Chapter 15	155
Chapter 16	167
Epilogue	173
Acknowledgments	177
About the Author	179

Foreword

JENNIFER GIMENEZ

As I read *Daughter of Korean Freud*, one saying kept ringing in my head: "We are only as sick as our secrets." This is a common phrase in recovery circles. It means that until we expose our secrets to the light, they can own us, fester within, and crush our souls.

Heawon could have kept her secrets and stayed silent. But thankfully, she didn't. Instead, she wrote a creative memoir that holds nothing back. Her heartbreaking, riveting story does more than expose the emotional, physical, and sexual traumas she endured. It also lays out how she processed and confronted those traumas. Along her healing path, she transforms from victim to victor, giving herself the same nurturing, compassion, and tough love that she provides for countless clients as a licensed psychotherapist.

Most victims of physical and sexual abuse suffer in silence. If you're one of them, you're not alone. One of five women in the US have been victims. Of those, many experience post-traumatic stress disorder, fall into alcohol or drug addictions to numb their pain, and struggle to build healthy relationships—all of which I did as a victim of sexual abuse. I kept my secrets hidden for years where my shame burned inside, leading me to addictions, mental health challenges, and a suicide attempt. I wish I'd applied the lessons from Heawon's story and gotten help, as she did, before my life unraveled.

Heawon's *Daughter of Korean Freud* is a provocative, gripping, well-told, and cathartic memoir about enduring emotional, physical, and sexual abuse in childhood while offering a road map for healing from trauma. While Heawon doesn't back away from telling her darkest secrets, she doesn't dwell on her traumas; rather, she finds a way forward. Eventually, while counseling a new client named Woo-ri, Heawon sees the parts of herself that still need to be repaired. Together, Heawon and Woo-ri learn to heal from their disturbing pasts, illustrating how recovery occurs in community with others. I felt like I walked with Heawon as she faced her past, searched her heart, and repaired her soul.

I repeat, if you've been a victim, you're not alone. And you don't need to stay stuck in the past or let the past keep you from a beautiful future. *Daughter of Korean Freud* can inspire you to find the healing you deserve.

Jennifer Gimenez
Supermodel, actor, and mental health/recovery activist

Introduction

Countless generations hear unsafe messages growing up:
"What happens in the family stays in the family."
"Never question authority figures."
"Loyalty means keeping our secrets."
"If you want my love and approval, you must do as I wish."

Parents and other authority figures often repeat words like these as mantras to hide a variety of dysfunctions. No matter what the victims do, they can't earn the approval and affection of their abusers. Instead, these victims are silenced.

I grew up in a family of social workers. Both of my parents earned degrees in social work. My father obtained his master's degree in the field, and during the 1980s, he grew so famous in South Korea that many in academia, government, and social work referred to him as the "Korean Freud." Although my mother quit her social work job after having children, she took pride in helping my father achieve that kind of success.

Despite my parents portraying an ideal image of our home life, my family held dark secrets.

Before leaving South Korea at age twenty-two, I earned my own degree in social work. Then I moved to the United States where I earned a master's degree at Adelphi University. During the last thirty years, I continued my education: doing post-graduate work at the Gestalt Center of Long Island, receiving certification for drug and alcohol recovery at the Pace School, and training in therapeutic acupuncture. My formal studies allowed me to apply psychotherapy to guide clients through their crises and traumas.

Several years into my private practice as a therapist, I met a client named Woo-ri, a young woman haunted by nightmares similar to mine. What secrets did our nightmares hold? What would our weekly sessions unearth about Woo-ri? What did I need to learn about myself? Could either of us find hope for a better future?

Standing on the shoulders of brave women and men who have come forward to share their life struggles, I have decided to make myself vulnerable by unmasking the story of my own abusive childhood. In doing so, I aim to offer hope to others who have lived through traumatic experiences by the hands of authority figures.

Daughter of Korean Freud is for those who have ever been abused, marginalized, or broken—and for those who were told to stay silent while these offenders took no responsibilities for their actions. The story is meant to assure you that emotional healing is possible, regardless of what life has thrown at you.

Chapter One

> *"This was the most Korean trait about her, her intense desire to die and survive at the same time, drives that didn't cancel each other."*
> —Cathy Park Hong, *In Minor Feelings*

When we met, I couldn't have known that Woo-ri, my new client, would meet with me for many years—always on Thursdays and at 4:00 p.m. precisely—nor that we would remain close like twins separated at birth.

First meetings with clients range from hit to miss. Over my three decades practicing as a psychotherapist, I've learned that some clients want a quick solution to a relatively minor problem, while others become regular fixtures on my couch. Usually, new clients want to see if therapy—or a particular therapist—feels like a good fit. Therapists are as plentiful as restaurants. You can get a meal on just about any corner, but something magical happens when you enter what becomes your new favorite place to eat.

I've also been honored that some clients have stayed for more than twenty years. Our relationships become something sacred, as we develop a trust like no other. I strive to meet my clients where they are in their journeys.

But Woo-ri didn't come to me via a referral from a current client. Rather, my former boss and dearest friend, Margherita, suggested I meet with Woo-ri.

"Of everyone I know, I think you'll relate with her and offer her the best outcome," Margherita told me at dinner one evening. "I hope you don't mind, but I already called your assistant to set up her first meeting with you next Thursday at 4:00 p.m. Will you please do this for me?"

Since Margherita served as my mentor, colleague, and friend, I could hardly say no.

Before I left that night, Margherita hugged me while saying, "Heawon, Woo-ri will be a gift to you as much as you are to her."

The afternoon that Woo-ri first breezed into my office, her seemingly young, attractive manner felt instantly familiar. And I got confirmation of an assumption I'd made when Margherita said her name was Woo-ri: *she's Korean.* Not that I only see Korean clients. I work with those from every ethnic group as well as various social and economic backgrounds. But since I'm Korean and fluent in both my language and English, many of my clients are Korean—telling me they find it easier to express complex thoughts and emotions in their native tongue. I also see several non-Koreans who have married Koreans. They choose me for my insights about the cultural nuances particular to Korean natives.

"Hello," I smiled warmly. "I'm so glad to meet you. Is it alright if I call you Woo-ri?"

"Yes, please," she answered. "And what would you like me to call you?" she asked, mindful of the respect for age and position in our Korean culture. We never assume that it's acceptable to call someone by their first name until we inquire.

"You can call me Heawon. Would you prefer that we speak English or Korean?" I asked.

"Korean, please."

"Good," I responded, extending my hand to her. Woo-ri met my right hand with hers and placed her left hand on her right wrist while bowing slightly—something that younger people would do to demonstrate respect for age and position rather than extending their hand first. These subtle formalities showed me that Woo-ri retained parts of our Korean culture.

Would you like to have a seat?" I asked, motioning to a chair and couch. "Anywhere you prefer is fine," I smiled.

Woo-ri turned quickly, her fashionable skirt and bobbed hair swirling around her as she spun and chose the plush leather sofa facing my chair, with my large office windows casting light from the side. Her face conveyed a blend of confidence and insecurity, similar to many of my clients. Sometimes called *false bravado,* Woo-ri's expression embodied the phrase, "Fake it till you make it."

Don't we all put on a strong front even when we're full of self-doubt? I thought to myself.

"Before we start, is there anything you want to ask about me, Woo-ri?"

"Yes, actually I do have a question. Is it true that you attended Yonsei University? I wanted to speak with a Korean. It's not easy to find a Korean therapist around here, especially one that attended Yonsei University, as they are a top college and known for having the best clinic."

"Well, yes, it's not easy to find a Korean therapist around. You came to the right place. I attended Yonsei University and had more training even after that."

"Very good then," she nodded.

"So Woo-ri, what brings you in today?" I asked.

"I want to talk about my recurring dream," Woo-ri said, taking charge of her session. "It disturbs me."

"Please," I offered. "I'd love to hear it."

Woo-ri looked up towards a picture on the wall behind me for a moment, pursing her lips slightly.

"Most of my dreams are absurd," she told me, embarrassment

flushing her cheeks. "Like I'm in a checkout line, but I can't find my purse. Or I'm back in school, and I don't speak the same language as everyone else. But this dream is different. I'm back on my honeymoon," she said, her voice dropping off.

"I see," I said, remembering what it felt like when I first moved to the US from Korea for graduate school. Even after studying English for years in high school and at the university, sitting in my first US lecture for my master's program, I listened for two hours without understanding a single word the professor spoke. I was terrified thinking about how I could complete my program without basic language skills. So when Woo-ri said she dreamed about not speaking the same language as those around her, I completely related. Dreams of feeling unprepared and ignorant are common in people suffering with anxiety.

"We flew to San Francisco after our wedding," Woo-ri looked far off. "October 17, 1989. We stayed at a luxurious place called the Huntington Hotel on Nob Hill, the highest place in San Francisco. My husband's parents paid for everything as our wedding gift. Our room from the tenth floor came with a breathtaking view of the Golden Gate Bridge through huge windows. "I'd just gone into the shower before getting dressed for dinner," she said matter-of-factly. "We had a reservation at the French restaurant downstairs."

Her face knotted as she continued.

"It was just after 5:00 p.m., I remember..." she said, her eyes looking darker. "Then the building began shaking," she said, growing more animated. "Boom! Boom! Boom! Loud noises cracked all around me. I ran out of the shower in a towel and saw the chandelier swaying from side to side while bouncing up and down like it was dancing. I wondered if the hotel was going to tip over or collapse on itself. The walls of our room buckled, and the paint cracked from the ceiling to partway down the wall. As the floor moved under my feet, I wobbled like I'd drunk too much *makgeolli*," she said, using the name of Korean rice wine. "The lights flickered and then went out. Outside I heard car alarms and loud popping noises.

"Just then, we heard a pounding at the door," she continued. "Then we heard screaming, 'It's an earthquake! Get out! Get out!' Hotel staff went to each door to evacuate the building.

"I threw on some clothes," she continued, talking more quickly as she replayed the events in her mind. "Out in the hallway, we saw many hotel guests running in both directions, many of them screaming. I watched an older couple standing in front of the elevator, pushing the button repeatedly, confused that the light wouldn't come on."

Woo-ri paused and peered over at the sky out my office window.

How terrible, I thought, waiting through her silence. I remembered that the earthquake had claimed many lives, wounded thousands, and damaged the San Francisco-Oakland Bay Bridge.

"We walked down the stairwell along with many other people," she continued. "By the time we got outside, the earth had stopped shaking. San Francisco has many hills, and I could see some smoke rising from the valley. Many buildings below had collapsed. Sounds of chaos surrounded us. Streets became gaping holes. Cars stopped, some of them half fallen into the open crevices created when the roads fell in."

My new client searched her memory, picturing every detail before continuing.

"Black smoke rose around us. Nob Hill is the highest part of the city, and since smoke rises, people covered their mouths as the air grew thick and noxious. Many were crying. Hours passed," she went on. "Eight o'clock, nine o'clock, ten o'clock. Darkness surrounded us, except for the flickering of fires burning below like a thick swarm of fireflies."

When Woo-ri paused, I sat still, willing her to continue.

"Then I saw an Asian man standing off by himself facing the bay," she continued, her eyes searching her mind as she recalled the vivid memory. "He did tai chi," she smiled and broke briefly from her story. "You know tai chi?"

"Yes," I said with a nod, fascinated as I pictured the scene.

"He moved in slow-motion, like he was underwater. Even with the sounds of sobbing and distant sirens echoing off the hotel building, this man had found a safe place inside his mind, as though he was unaffected by the turmoil. *He's right to ignore the chaos,* I thought to myself. This made me realize, *so what if I die? I've practiced dying my entire life. Why should I be afraid now?*" she concluded with a slight shrug before shifting her eyes back to me.

I've practiced dying my entire life, I repeated her enigmatic statement in my mind. *What does that mean?* I wondered. I didn't speak immediately. Instead, I let Woo-ri's words hang in the air.

"Can you say more about what you mean by practicing dying your entire life?" I asked, finally breaking the silence. "I want to make sure that I understand you."

Instead of answering, Woo-ri chewed on her bottom lip while looking off past my head again.

"I don't think you can help me," she answered at last while shaking her head. "I think I'm too far gone."

So began my first session with Woo-ri, a young woman who would ultimately surprise me by forcefully awakening the dormant parts of my own life that I'd never processed.

Chapter Two

"[T]here is something indestructible at the center of each of us; though the pain of being transformed and rearranged while still alive often feels unbearable."
—Mark Nepo, *The Book of Awakening*

"What else did she say?" Margherita asked me an hour later over dinner at her home.

I treat my counseling relationships as sacrosanct and confidential, meaning I've never shared clients' names or specific details with friends. But Margherita was beyond a friend. She'd hired me as a therapist shortly after I completed graduate school in the US. Since that time, she'd worn multiple hats in our relationship: therapist, supervisor, friend, and surrogate mother. Besides, Margherita had suggested I spend some time with Woo-ri, and I put my utmost trust in her while brainstorming about certain clients.

"I asked her what she meant by that, that she'd been *practicing dying her whole life*, but she changed the subject," I responded between bites of salad. "Actually, what she said next was something like, 'I don't think you can help me.'"

"Does she seem *suicidal*?" Margherita asked, a bit concerned.

"No," I answered quickly, shaking my head to reinforce my answer.

My eyes fell onto the black-rimmed, white-faced clock mounted on her kitchen wall. The second hand jerked in place around the ten as if it lacked the energy to make it to the twelve before gravity alone would pull it down again to the other side.

"At least not now," I added, pulling my mind back to the topic. "But I get a sense that she's had thoughts of death in the past, if not suicide attempts or suicidal ideations."

I knew that thoughts of death would often precede thoughts of taking one's own life. Neither indirect, vague suicidal statements nor direct threats, nor recurring thoughts of death should be ignored in a client. But I sensed in Woo-ri a strong, underlying resilience, almost a defiance to live despite any negative events she might have experienced. Still, I felt relief when Woo-ri scheduled another appointment before leaving my office. I would see her again at 4 p.m. the following Thursday, and I believed I would have time to unwrap her mystery.

"I'm sure you'll learn more when you delve into her past," Margherita offered with confidence. "What do you know of her family history?"

I placed a hand over my mouth and one finger of my other hand in the air while I finished chewing. Once I swallowed, I responded to her question. "She doesn't wish to speak about her family. She wants to focus on her honeymoon only—her recurring, upsetting dream."

"So she wasn't scared of the earthquake," Margherita said aloud. "Is that why she didn't seem afraid of it? Because she's been anticipating her death?"

"I haven't gotten that far with her yet," I shrugged. "But I asked what she thought her recurring dream meant."

"I hate to interrupt," Margherita jumped in, "but do you get the sense that what she shared was just a dream? Or did that really happen to her?"

I shrugged again. "I think the honeymoon and the earthquake happened, but it's likely that her dream embellished some details?" I said this as a question, not sure of the answer.

"Okay," Margherita nodded. "Sorry for the rabbit trail. So what did she think her dream meant?"

I sipped some wine before answering.

"She thinks it was a sign that her marriage wasn't meant to be," I answered.

"Is that what she thought *then*? Or is that what she now believes based on hindsight?" Margherita wanted to know.

"I don't know," I shook my head from side to side. "By the time she finished telling me about her nightmare, I didn't have time for many follow-up questions," I added, wondering if I had mismanaged my time with Woo-ri and offered her nothing more than a supportive ear. "But she said the earthquake gave her confirmation that her marriage was doomed to fail and not meant to be."

"Interesting," Margherita said in a tone that indicated she thought there might be more to my client's story. "Well, your client's in great hands," she said with a wink. "I know you two will get to the bottom of things. You said that you will see her again, right?"

"Yes," I smiled. "Next Thursday at 4:00 pm, right before I come here for dinner. Oh wait, next week it's my turn to cook," I remembered as we both laughed.

"Just make something delicious," Margherita laughed again. "And if you find yourself running late next week, please don't hurry because of me. I know where you keep your spare key. I'll let myself in and open a bottle of wine while I wait," she smiled supportively.

I don't know where the rest of the evening went. I sat on the couch in my living room, without reading or watching television. I remember thinking at one point that it had gotten dark outside.

The next thing I knew, the clock on my phone told me I'd been sitting in the dark well past my bedtime.

I quickly completed my bedtime routine and slid in under my bedspread. But my mind refused to turn off. Instead of sleeping, I spent hours flailing around like I was Jacob wrestling with God.

I should have expected my restlessness. Whenever I spoke Korean in therapy, a switch flipped in my mind, as if the act of reverting to my native language rebooted my brain to *all things* Korean—like how Proust wrote about the taste of madeleines dipped in tea creating an involuntary recall of long-forgotten events.

I spent the first twenty-two years of my life in South Korea, and the imprint of my formative years never left me. As I tossed in bed, I subconsciously wrinkled my nose as I remembered the smells of the nearly tropical summers in South Korea. Overflowing sewers, stale cigarettes, car exhaust, and *gochujang*, a pungent Korean paste made from red chilis, rice, and fermented soybeans. But when the season turned to fall and early winter, even within the city of Seoul, I often escaped into the Bukhansan, Dobongsan, or Suraksan mountains to savor the sweet scent of pine—and in certain months, soak in their splendor as their dark, patterned needles peeked out from the fog or snow.

And the food! Even as I've stretched my palate to include foods from around the world, I still dreamed of kimchi loaded with *gochugaru*, spring onions, garlic, and ginger. The foods I grew up with remained my go-to comfort foods. I craved *haejang-guk* (hangover soup), *tteokbokkias* (spicy rice cakes), and hardboiled eggs marinated in soy sauce, garlic, and Japanese rice wine when I wanted to reconnect to the most enduring, positive parts of my earlier years.

Then of course, I pictured my friends—specifically Chang Min, my first real love. I could still see his lovely face, and my mind returned to the discotheque where several of my college classmates held a party. On the dance floor, a boy I wasn't interested in grabbed me to dance. I pulled away quickly, and in doing so, nearly bowled over Chang Min, who held me to keep me from falling.

"I'm so sorry," I gushed, looking up at his attractive face and soft eyes.

"Anytime," he smiled, still holding me as if I might drop should he let go.

Don't let go, I whispered to him with my mind.

I tried to straighten myself without separating my body from his touch. Chang smiled back, his strong fingers and arms relaxing around my shoulders until they felt like an intimate embrace. My body tingled.

"Thank you," I said coyly, not sure what to say—or what to make of the feelings that heated up my insides.

"Well, since we're already on the dance floor," he laughed easily while motioning to the bodies in motion around us, "would you like to dance?"

"Oh, yes," I gushed, immediately wishing I hadn't sounded so eager.

But I was. And I soon learned that Chang felt strongly attracted to me.

While we talked through the night, I found that every part of Chang made my heart race. First, Chang was gorgeous. I know I said that he was attractive, but that's an understatement. His cheeks and jaw seemed sculpted from granite. In his almond eyes, I read both kindness and deep intelligence.

Second, when he spoke, his words and depth told me he had the mind of a scholar. He'd read philosophy, theology, economics, politics, and psychology. He could weave one topic into the next, like beads of water melding to form a singular puddle.

Third, like me, Chang studied social work at Yonsei University. When he completed school, he would apply his caring soul to helping others. The clincher came when he told me his post-graduate plans.

"When I finish school here, I'm going to the United States to further my studies," Chang told me.

"Me, too!" I said with glee and disbelief.

"Really?" he asked, a bit surprised.

"Yes," I repeated, "to all of it! I'm studying social work, and I want to continue my studies in the US too!"

From that evening on, Chang and I grew inseparable. Even though we attended a very large university, we became the "it" couple on campus. Other students, especially those in social services, knew us and admired what we shared.

"They're moving to America," I overheard a girl gossip about us as Chang and I, hand in hand, walked through the quad.

"I'm not surprised," her friend replied. "They already have it all here. They need a bigger pond."

Yes, we do have it all, I thought to myself, thrilled that I had begun to shake off the insecurities that had plagued me since childhood.

A house-shaking rumble followed immediately by a bright flash of lightning shook me back to my present—alone at night in bed. So entranced by the memories of my true love, I hadn't noticed the storm gathering outside. Now that my attention returned to my room, I heard the wind slapping rain against my huge windows. A low moan whispered from under the eaves, and the storm blew through the small holes of the soffit, creating a sound like wailing bagpipes.

I rolled onto my other side, eager to return to my in-bed daydream about Chang.

"What is he studying?" I remembered my mom asking me as we sat at the kitchen table in my family's South Korean home.

"Social work," I smiled. "Just like me. Just like you and dad," I added in hopes of earning her approval.

"Hmph," my mom vocalized. "Does he come from money?"

"His father is a businessman," I answered.

"Is he Protestant?" my mom continued to probe as if looking

for a reason why Chang and I could not be together.

"No," I said slowly. "He is a Catholic. But I've already told him that I'm willing to convert to Catholicism so we can be married in his church. I'm going to take confirmation classes."

Mom looked off into the next room. After shifting in her chair, she stared into my eyes again.

"So what's wrong with him?" she asked.

"There's nothing wrong with him," I said quickly. "We want the same things in life, and we care about each other a lot."

"Why is he interested in you?" Mom replied, emphasizing the word *you*.

"Mom," I started to protest.

"Does he think we have money? Or that your father can help him get ahead in his career?"

"Mom," I said again before forcing myself to stop.

"Are you sure he doesn't already have a girlfriend?" she pushed.

"No, Mom!" I said defiantly. "He *had* a girlfriend, but they broke up months ago. He loves *me*, no one else." My voice trailed off as my ability to defend myself waned.

"Ah!" she said as if she'd discovered my weak spot. "So, he has a girlfriend and is just having fun with you!" she said victoriously.

"That's not true, Mom," I answered, trying to remain calm. "They broke up *months* ago."

"If he's really broken up with his last girlfriend, he needs to tell her that he is not interested in seeing her again ever," my mom demanded. "What's to keep her from coming back into his life?"

"He's had that conversation with her, Mom," I said weakly. "That's what *broken up* means. They are no longer together."

"He needs to end it with her completely, leaving no room for her to get back into his life," she said with conviction. "If not, she might come back and say, 'He's my boyfriend, not yours.' And then she will haunt you!"

Neither the Christian nor Korean traditions warned of *hauntings* when a man failed to seal off a former girlfriend with the cement of a sharp, cold renunciation. But my mother insisted that it must be done.

Even though I found my mother's demand absurd, I respected her wishes. Although I didn't do this out of true respect; instead, I did it to get her off my back in hopes she wouldn't interfere in my relationship with Chang. So I relayed her words to Chang.

"Sure, no problem," Chang responded kindly. "If that'll make your mother happy, I'll do it."

Little did Chang know that making Mom happy was an impossibility.

"You're the only one I love," he shrugged. "So yeah, I'll go see my ex to make sure she knows that I am completely in love with you and that she and I will never be together again."

Chang spoke to his ex-girlfriend.

"What did she say?" I asked, eager to make sure that they were completely done, even though I had no reason to doubt Chang's assurances. *Thanks for making me suspicious, Mother,* I thought.

"Well," Chang laughed, "she laughed in my face. She told me, 'Duh, that's what broken up means. We shared a past but not a future.' So tell your mom that I'm all yours!"

"That's so embarrassing," I cringed, picturing how awkward that must have been for him, and then I gave him a big hug. "I'm so sorry that my mom insisted that you talk to her. But at least we won't be haunted by her evil spirit!" I laughed as Chang joined in.

After months of hearing me gush about Chang each night at home, my father decided that he needed to meet Chang himself before giving his blessing to our relationship. Mother, on the other hand, didn't join us for dinner. I'd grown to accept that my mom felt little maternal love for me. She treated me like she was an unhappy, distant relative who had been pressed into caring for me, her ungrateful and horrible ward, out of familial duty and at great personal sacrifice to her own dreams.

Chang and I met my dad at an American restaurant. My dad walked in carrying a single red rose and presented it to Chang.

Again, this little token didn't line up with either American or Korean cultures, but I think my dad thought his gesture seemed cool. I figured maybe he'd seen this in an American movie, but he got confused and played the part of the lover instead of the father.

"Well," my father said, appraising Chang as if he were a side of beef, "let me get a good look at you."

Chang smiled good-naturedly and spread his arms wide. I'm pretty sure if he weren't seated, he'd have twirled so my dad could take in the whole view.

"OK," Dad said at last. "Once I find out what kind of boy you are, I can give you my approval," he announced with a wink.

By the end of dinner, Dad was won over.

"You seem highly intelligent, kind, and quite grounded," my dad told Chang. "So the two of you have my consent to continue seeing each other and to pursue marriage if you choose."

I squeezed Chang's hand underneath the table.

Once I had father's blessing, I had one final obstacle to marrying Chang. I'd finished my confirmation classes already, but I needed to complete the two sacraments to join the Catholic Church: confirmation and baptism. Finally, these two sacraments were within reach to mark off on my pre-marriage checklist.

But the morning of the Church ceremony for my conversion to Catholicism, I fell ill.

"What's wrong?" my mother asked with annoyance.

"I'm sick," I moaned. "I feel hot."

Cold sweat pooled on my skin. After taking my temperature, I understood why I felt so dizzy and miserable. My fever read 102° F. I quickly called Chang.

"I'm so sorry," I slurred into the phone. "I'm sick."

A short time later, Chang came to see me. He sat by my side, holding a cool cloth to my head.

"I wish I could make you feel better," he told me. "You feel very hot."

"I don't want to miss the confirmation and baptism," I cried to him.

"Shhhhh," he soothed me. "Just feel better. You can complete things with the Church another time. For now, just get some rest and let your body fight off your fever."

After a few days, my fever left. I returned to school and rescheduled my confirmation. When I told Chang the good news, he returned with some news of his own.

"That's wonderful," he beamed. "And I have some great news on my end, too: my parents want to meet your parents over dinner. Since we will soon begin our final year at university, they are excited to give us their blessing for our marriage."

Marriage! I could barely contain my joy and anticipation. *How could I have ever won the love of someone as charismatic, handsome, and brilliant like Chang?* I wondered.

Chang adored me and called me beautiful. He saw me for who I was, loving me and never judging me. *Am I really going to marry my forever love, move to the United States, and start life again with my beloved?* I wondered. It felt too good to be true.

When our families met at the restaurant, my heart overflowed with excitement. After everyone bowed and introduced themselves around the table, Chang's father spoke to my dad.

"I understand that you've earned a master's in social work," he said. "That must be fascinating work."

"Yes," my father nodded in appreciation. "I've been fortunate enough to work for the good of South Korean families," my father answered modestly.

"I understand from Heawon that you've been instrumental in creating policies for the betterment of all of South Korea," Chang's father continued with true admiration.

"Enough about me," my father humbly changed the subject. "You are a businessman," he said.

"Yes, I'm grateful to have many happy customers," he smiled and nodded as I noted how much Chang resembled his father. "I'm fortunate enough to offer meaningful employment to many people as my own way of helping South Korea. Of course, what I do is nothing compared to your work," he added.

The mutual admiration between the two men continued throughout dinner. Chang and I shared smiles with one another in silent acknowledgement of how well our families got along.

After saying our goodbyes, I returned home with my mom and dad, feeling fulfilled, excited, and full of anticipation.

But those feelings didn't last long. After we arrived at home, my mother took to her bed and refused to get up. The next day, she refused food.

"What's wrong, Mother?" I asked. "Please get up and eat," I encouraged her.

"That woman disrespected me," she said as she rolled over away from me.

"What do you mean?" I asked, astonished by her words. "What woman?"

"Don't pretend you didn't hear it," she snapped. "Chang's mother thinks she is better than me, better than all of us. She's controlling, and she wants to control our family."

"Mom," I shook my head as tears rushed to my eyes, "I didn't hear anything like that. What did she say? If she said something offensive, please tell me what it was."

"I will not repeat it," my mother said as she pulled the blanket over her head.

A moment later, from under the blanket, she added, "But I cannot approve of your marriage to Chang. I refuse to be anyone's slave."

Sitting next to her, I let my tears fall on her blanket. I wept for what I knew would be the first of many more tears to come as the initial shock of grief overtook me. Deeper, darker grief would come later, forcing me to detach from my emotions lest I tear the flesh off my bones.

My dad was in the living room, which was right next their bedroom. He heard my interactions with Mom, and he didn't intervene. He didn't even lift his face to see how I was. He just kept reading, or pretended to read, whatever book he had in front of him.

This is how it ends, I knew. *Mom's narcissistic manipulation means I must let go of Chang. Even if I were to marry Chang and move away, she would do everything in her power to control our lives at every turn. She would starve herself for a week or longer, waiting for me to cave to her demands. I couldn't let Chang experience such pain because of my mother's sickness or because of me. It's better that I hurt him now instead of devastating him later,* I told myself.

It's funny, I thought. *As much as I hate my mom for doing this, I can't stand the thought of letting her starve herself. Even when she is hateful and controlling of me, I still want to protect her as much as I want to protect Chang.*

The next day, I did what must be done. I created some story to tell Chang. I don't remember what I said. Even while I sat with him at the coffee shop, I felt like I watched the two of us from outside my body. I'm sure whatever came out of my mouth made no sense to him, because I didn't understand it myself. Even as I spoke, I couldn't hear my own voice. I also don't know what emotion registered across Chang's beautiful face, because I couldn't look at him. My mind blocked out all memory of those cruel moments and the despair I experienced over the next several months.

By the time I left the coffee shop, no feelings remained inside of me. I'd gone numb, dead. One lone thought kept me going*: I need to get out of my house as soon as possible.*

When my alarm sounded the next morning, my face and pillow were soaked. I couldn't distinguish between the memories I'd brought back to the forefront of my mind and the dream I may have had the night before, even when I thought sleep had evaded me.

Chapter Three

> "Traumatic stress can spread to anyone with whom the
> sufferers share their lives. Trauma begets trauma."
> —Shaili Jain, *The Unspeakable Mind*

My half-awake dreams of the night didn't dissolve with the daylight. They stayed with me throughout my morning run. Having worked so hard to put the unpleasantness of my past behind me, my life somehow felt inexplicably connected with the story of Woo-ri, even after one brief session together.

Our troubles from the past can walk with us into the future, I knew. I'd seen this in my clients. I'd seen this in myself.

The suburban scenery around my Nassau County home blurred as I jogged the streets. But instead of seeing manicured lawns and colorful gardens, I saw the smog of Seoul—a city crowded with people, car exhaust, and traffic rushing past me in a colorless haze.

Having spent my formative years in a different country than the one I now enjoyed, I learned that culture reaches beyond the foods I enjoy, the color of my hair, and the shape of my eyes. My

Korean culture lived inside each cell of my body whenever my mind returned to old, painful memories.

Driving to work later that morning, I realized that I couldn't wait until my Thursday appointment with Woo-ri. She connected me to my Korean heritage. Even though I'd seen hundreds of Korean clients in my practice over the years, Woo-ri's matter-of-fact statement that she'd been planning her entire life to die summarized my childhood unlike any other comments a client had expressed to me.

Do her words speak for me, too? I considered. *As a child in South Korea, had I been awaiting, almost anticipating, my own death?*

As a professional skilled at compartmentalizing my personal life from my counseling profession, I shrugged off the last thoughts about my past as I walked through the office door. For the next few days, I met with many clients, plugging into their needs while offering them meaningful guidance and emotional support so they could take steps necessary for their tough journeys. In the evenings, I spent time with my friends or books, and sometimes went on a second run for the day.

But Wednesday evening, I broke my routine. After a light dinner, I sat in my living room thinking about how I might best approach my next meeting with Woo-ri. *Rapport isn't built on demand*, I told myself. Most clients would take time to trust me with their secrets and their fears. Instead of forcing the therapeutic relationship, I'd encourage each client to set their own pace, neither prematurely forcing them into personal discovery nor sitting idly like an extension of the furniture. I tried to remain open and receptive to whatever they might share with me, letting psychological safety evolve at its own pace.

I felt like I got to know Woo-ri from our first meeting better than I'd gotten to know some clients after a half-dozen sessions. Just like hearing a song from your formative years can bring back memories from that time, speaking to another South Korean in our native language seemed to fixate me on my own childhood memories.

What more must I know if I'm to help her explore the haunting yet ambiguous nature of her nightmare? I wondered as I took a small sip of a deep, rich cabernet. *And how can I guard against interpreting events from Woo-ri's life based on my own personal experiences?*

I wrote a short list of questions that I'd ask Woo-ri when the time seemed right. Once I finished making notes, I zipped my leather-bound notebook closed and sat in the sunroom overlooking my backyard where many different birds, deer, squirrels, rabbits, and groundhogs would run around looking for food or playing together as daylight turned to dusk and into night.

"Hello, Woo-ri," I said warmly as I opened the door connecting my office to the waiting room. "It is so good to see you again. Please, come in."

As I held the door open, Woo-ri breezed into my office, her white, cinch-waisted dress seemingly painted with an assortment of colorful polka dots blurring behind her. Then she plopped down in the same place she'd sat the previous week.

"Before we start, I want to tell you how much I love your dress!" I gushed sincerely. "I used to have a similar one."

"Thank you," she smiled at the compliment. "It might have been yours. I got it at a secondhand boutique!" She laughed at her own comment, and I joined her.

"How has your week been so far?" I asked, easing into our session.

"It's been good," Woo-ri answered definitively. I waited a few beats to see if she'd add more, but her silence told me that she had no interest in recapping her week with small talk. I decided to jump straight in.

"Well, Woo-ri, the last time we met, you told me about your

recurring nightmare...About the earthquake while you were on your honeymoon," I summarized. "You mentioned that you saw a man doing tai chi in the middle of the chaos and that you felt like you'd been preparing to die your entire life."

Woo-ri nodded her head slightly before pushing herself into the back of the couch and the armrest. She twisted her body sideways and drew her legs up close to her chest, locking her hands around her shins.

"Was this a dream, or was this something that actually happened?" I asked.

"It was both," Woo-ri replied. "I still dream about what happened that night. I've had that dream several times, like my mind replays it."

"Why do you think you're still having that dream?" I asked. "I'm sorry, first let me ask, how long ago was that event?"

"It's been about twenty years," she answered.

I couldn't have worked at a carnival guessing people's ages. I would have guessed Woo-ri to be in her early twenties, and from her yoga-like position on my sofa, she could well have been a teenager.

"I see," I said, realizing that she must be around my age. "Do you feel like you have some unresolved conflict from that time in your life?"

"Unresolved, like how?" she answered with her own question.

"I don't know," I shrugged. "I'm wondering why the nightmare has come back to you now, especially after so many years. Maybe it would help if you told me what happened next?"

"Okay," Woo-ri answered, her eyes shifting slightly to the left as she accessed her memory.

"My dream stops there," she said. "Right after I saw the man practicing tai chi. But I can tell you what happened next in my life if it's helpful."

"Yes, that would be helpful," I said encouragingly.

"After the earthquake ended, the staff came outside and told us that we could return to our rooms at our own risk," she said. "What did I care? I had no fear of death. I told my husband, 'Well, if we're going to die, we might as well die in a soft bed.'" She laughed a bit as she recalled her conversation.

"I fell asleep right away," Woo-ri said. "Since even before our wedding day, we'd been go, go, go. So, I was tired. While I slept, my husband had been trying to make plans to get us out of San Francisco and back to New York. The next morning, he told me that we needed to get to the airport so we could fly standby. So we packed our things and went to the airport. Since we hadn't eaten since lunch the day before, we went downstairs for breakfast. Nothing ever ruins my appetite," she smiled. "But you know, we don't have earthquakes in Korea."

"Or New York!" I added with a laugh.

"Right!" she laughed. "So, I didn't know anything about aftershakes. Is that what they're called?"

"Maybe aftershocks?" I asked, not sure of the word myself.

"Yes, aftershocks," Woo-ri nodded. "But the people in the restaurant must have known all about them. Every several minutes, the ground would shake a bit. I saw a man walking from the breakfast counter when a shake hit. I had to stop myself from laughing. A sausage bounced off his plate and onto the floor!" she laughed for several moments as she relived the memory. "He looked at it, shook his head, and then went back to get another sausage. To him, this was nothing but a small inconvenience."

"When we got back to New York, everyone in his family joked with us, saying things like, 'Your marriage started on shaky ground.' Because it had, literally.

"Next we found a house that we loved. His parents helped us with a down payment. My apartment had been a one-hour drive to work—two hours driving each day. That was a lot, but after we moved into the new house, I spent five hours commuting by train each day to and from work. When it rained or snowed, it could take as long as seven hours. And the train station in Jamaica," she added, referencing a stop in Queens before switching gears, "Do you know it?"

"Yes, I've ridden that train line before," I nodded sympathetically.

"It's a dangerous area with people selling drugs, and I'd see violence every day," she sighed. "Just to get to and from work, I felt like I had to go through a war zone."

"How about your husband?" I asked. "How was his commute?"

"He worked in the wealthiest part of Long Island with an hour drive each way," Woo-ri said.

"Did your long commute bother you?" I asked.

"Yes, it did. It reminded me of high school where I spent the same amount of time commuting. At any rate, once we got married, I started thinking that I was working much harder than he was. I thought we should both work hard to get ahead so we could earn the best life, you know?"

"Do you mean he wasn't a hard worker? Like you, I mean?" I asked.

"He worked for a real estate law practice," Woo-ri said. "Very prestigious job. But..." her voice trailed off.

I waited her out.

"We kept our accounts separate until after we were married," she shook her head. "Only once we put our money in the same account did I learn that he made about the same as I made. So even with both of our salaries, we did not have much."

"Did it bother you that he didn't make as much money as you thought he did?" I asked.

"I worked so hard for everything," her face filled with anger. "To attend university, make good grades, get a good job. And then after we got married, do you know what he told me?"

I waited out her rhetorical question.

"An actor," she spit out. "He wanted to be an actor! He came from a wealthy family, got an elite education and a law degree, worked for a successful company, yet had no money. So he had all of this potential, but he wanted to throw away everything so he could be an actor!"

I listened and let a long pause come between us.

"I thought he was my Daddy Long Legs," she said in a sad voice.

As a child, I'd read *Daddy Long Legs* by Jean Webster, the story of a young orphan who received charity from an anonymous benefactor to pay for her college education. Later, the orphan marries her no-longer unknown savior, who is a wealthy, older man. I spent much of my youth wondering why I couldn't find my own Daddy Long Legs who would take me from Korea and lead me to the promised land of the US.

*I'd met him. His name was Chang. But...*I remembered before returning to Woo-ri.

"It sounds like you felt disappointed, maybe even betrayed by your husband?" I asked for clarification.

"Yes, but that makes me feel bad," she said in a conflicted tone. "He'd been very good to me when we dated," Woo-ri said, wiping her eyes. "He was perfect in nearly every way."

"What does that mean to you? *Perfect*?"

"He did pro bono work for refugees and had such a good heart. He cared about them a lot and helped them get legal status in America. He became my friend. But that's what he was, a friend. When I needed a car, he helped me find one that I could afford. And he loved Korean food," Woo-ri smiled, "which was nice. He came from a great family, and like me, he was a Christian. He even went to a Korean church with me."

"It sounds like you loved him for many reasons," I reflected when she finished talking.

"On paper, he was perfect for me, yes," she nodded. "He even played the guitar and sang with me while I played the piano. We had so many things in common," she shook her head. "But he wasn't driven like me. Everything in his life had been handed to him, so he didn't understand working hard to get ahead in life. He didn't understand the Asian way."

I understood. In South Korea, a country with more people than opportunities, doors wouldn't fly open. If you want to set yourself apart from the crowd, you had to distinguish yourself, which often meant studying all the time instead of having a balanced life. I traveled hours to school in high school, then in college. Nothing came quickly or easily for me. I needed to study constantly. I even attended school on the weekend for extra help, yet I still felt it wasn't enough.

"Then one weekend, we were sitting in the backyard...beautiful day, blue sky, flowers blooming, no bugs, full sun. But I got upset with him for no reason. He wasn't doing anything. And I blew our weekend," Woo-ri said. "I told him, 'We need to work harder to make our life better. We need to make more progress than we're making today.'"

"What did he say to that?"

"Nothing," Woo-ri shrugged. "He made a face, like a frown, and one of his eyebrows shot up," Woo-ri answered, followed by silence. "Then I shut down."

"What made you shut down, do you think?" I prodded.

"The look on his face was the same one my brother used to show me," she said, shifting her body until she turned her profile to me.

"Say more about your brother," I said, intrigued, as I considered my own abusive brother.

"My husband had done so much for me," Woo-ri continued, ignoring my question. "He helped me over and over. After graduate school, my visa ran out. He took care of all the legal work on my behalf. I should have loved him despite everything," Woo-ri said, showing her inner conflict.

"I thought maybe our problem was cultural. Me, a poor South Korean girl, and he, a Cornell-educated lawyer from a wealthy family. I thought he must not understand how the rest of the world lived, since he seemed to take his privilege and opportunity so lightly," she added.

After a pause, she continued. "Shortly after we married, I met this nice Korean man at a work function. And I spent the whole time speaking in Korean with him, sharing stories about our shared culture. When I got home, I told my husband about my new Korean friend. Then he asked, 'Well, if you can have a male friend, can I have a female friend?'"

"What did you say to him?" I asked.

"Of course not!" Woo-ri said with emphasis. "He had plenty of Americans he could speak English with and talk about America. But besides church, I had no Korean friends."

Makes sense on one level, I thought, *but what about what he needed and wanted in his life?* I wondered as I scratched a note on my pad.

"We didn't have a terrible life together. We went to work, ate dinner, talked, played cards," she listed off the activities the two of them shared. "But I was getting tired. I wanted to get ahead, to get to a place where we could do more than pay our bills."

"Besides him wanting to stop practicing law to pursue acting, what other friction points did you have in your relationship?" I asked.

Instead of answering my question directly, Woo-ri repeated what she had said in our previous session.

"When the earthquake came, I knew what it meant," she said looking far off. "I shouldn't have married him. Did I marry him out of guilt for all that he'd done for me and the hope of what more he might be able to do for me? Or did I marry him because marriage seemed the next logical step in our relationship and my life? I don't know. But I feel bad now, because I know that he loved me deeply. But I didn't know how to love him for who he was," she lowered her head. "I married the idea of my Daddy Long Legs, my Prince Charming. But I didn't love my husband, the man I married," she finished in a soft voice.

I glanced at the clock behind Woo-ri's head, and I couldn't believe that our time had gone over. Since she was my last client of the day, I didn't have anyone waiting, but I wanted to provide her with some closure on this session before letting her go.

"Do you think you feel some guilt from marrying him? Do you think that's why you keep having the earthquake nightmare?" I asked.

"I kept thinking there was something lacking in our sexual intimacy," she said, not seeming to answer my question directly. "I couldn't pinpoint what it was, since I was not experienced in sex. Also, I felt damaged because of my history from childhood."

"What do you mean by your history?"

Woo-ri looked almost blank at this question. So I asked a different question.

"If he were here in this room right now, what would you want to be able to say to him?"

"I would tell him that he did nothing wrong," Woo-ri said, tears this time falling down her cheeks. "I would tell him that my feelings, or lack of feelings, about him was about me, not him."

Then she stood up and left without another word.

I don't think I've even scratched the surface on her story, I admitted to myself.

Chapter Four

> *"We are all controlled by the world we live in...*
> *The question is this: are we to be controlled by*
> *accidents, by tyrants, or by ourselves?"*
> —B.F. Skinner

Since it was my turn to host the regular Thursday-night dinner with Margherita, once I got home, I quickly prepared chicken cordon bleu, braised brussels sprouts, and quinoa with herbs. After placing full, hot plates in front of Margherita's and my place settings, I asked her if I could talk about my client, Woo-ri.

"Remember her recurring nightmare about the earthquake on her honeymoon? Well, that actually happened," I told Margherita between bites. "What I haven't been able to figure out is why she's having these nightmares now, nearly twenty years later."

"I'm guessing you asked her, and she doesn't know?" Margherita asked.

"She's not sure what's triggered her dreams," I nodded, "but I think she's holding onto to multiple layers of guilt, shame, and anger. Time will tell what she will share with me."

We ate in comfortable silence for a few moments. Our friendship was such that we could talk about anything or nothing and enjoy our time together immensely.

"Although she hasn't mentioned anything concrete, I wonder what role her family may have played in her anxiety," I said after a period of silence. "At our last meeting, she told me how she had become triggered by a look in her husband's eyes that reminded her of how her brother used to look at her."

"What did she say about her brother?"

"Well, just that. She and her husband were starting to get into an intense discussion, and then she said something like, 'He made a face like my brother used to make.' So I'm sure what happened after her brother made that face at her must have traumatized her. Odd and significant, don't you think?"

"Absolutely. You expect abuse?" Margherita skipped straight to the point.

"I'm assuming," I said in a non-committal tone, "but I know nothing for certain."

"How old did you say she is?" she asked between bites.

"I don't know her exact age, but her honeymoon was twenty years ago. She looks very young," I added.

"So do you, Heawon!" Margherita said with a chuckle. "I should have such good genes!"

We shared a laugh together, which reminded me of a story from my childhood that I wanted to share to transition into a lighter topic.

"I told you that my father worked closely with the American Red Cross and other service organizations, right?" I asked, not sure if I'd mentioned that to her before.

"Yes, I think I remember you saying that."

"Because of that, my father distributed food, clothes, books, and other donated items to care for the neediest in South Korea. Throughout my childhood, my father stored boxes full of items in the attic before they got distributed. Well, one day I snuck into the attic when nobody was home, and I looked through some of the boxes just to see what was in them. I found this box full of American cookies. They looked so good that I just had to open the box. Once I took a cookie out of the box, I convinced myself that I should eat one, since I was hungry and there were so many cookies left," I giggled as Margherita's face showed that she could picture the temptation of Heawon.

"Then I took a bite," I paused and made a face of ecstasy. "I'd never tasted something so wonderful. I'd expected it to be sweet like most American treats. But this tasted almost savory. You know what they say about potato chips, how you can't eat just one? Well, I couldn't stop after the first treat. I ate the whole box! I swear I didn't mean to! Then I felt so guilty that I hid the empty box and promised myself that I'd never again open Pandora's tasty box of guilt upon myself!"

We laughed again.

"Have you found those cookies since you moved here? I mean, you could eat all you want now with absolutely no guilt!" Margherita laughed loudly.

"I did, I did!" I exclaimed. "In fact, I bought some the other day. Let me grab the box!"

I retrieved the box from the pantry and handed it to Margherita.

She looked at the box for a moment, and then put on her reading glasses that she kept on a chain around her neck.

"Heawon!" she exclaimed. "These are dog biscuits!"

"Hahaha, I know that now, but I didn't back then!" I said as we both laughed. "I promise that I don't eat them any longer. I got those for my dog, Paduki. He loves them as much as I did as a child!"

"Thank God!" Margherita laughed again. "Because if this is what you planned for dessert, I'd have to pass!"

After Margherita left, I let my internal darkness embrace me. Thanks to Margherita, Paduki, and a handful of other friends, I rarely felt alone these days. While my husband, Miguel, often spent a lot of time each year abroad for work, I could count on his family for love and support, especially during his absence. I reflected on how I'd gotten to this point.

I'd met Miguel shortly after divorcing my first husband, Asper.

I couldn't help but think of Asper whenever I thought about Miguel. All my relationships seemed connected by a gossamer thread stemming back to my Korean roots and my first love, Chang.

I met Asper through a Vietnamese man named Hong while working an internship at a refugee center. Hong was a lawyer working at a Catholic agency who also helped the refugees. Hong looked so much like Chang that I couldn't take my eyes off him. When Hong invited me to a BBQ at his parents' house, I eagerly accepted, picturing myself with Hong as if Chang were once again in my life. At the BBQ, Hong's friend Asper introduced himself to me. Asper was a very tall, thin American with Irish heritage.

Even though I attended the BBQ because I was irrationally attracted to a Vietnamese Chang, Hong wasn't to be part of my future. Asper, though, became a close friend and eventual husband.

I grew to care about Asper as we spent more time together. How couldn't I? He was well educated, kind, patient, and cultured. Since I'd been in the country only a year when I met him, I still struggled with English. Asper came to my rescue, helping me write papers for my graduate studies at Adelphi University. On weekends, Asper expanded my cultural horizons by taking me to musicals, plays, Broadway shows, and fine restaurants. Through Asper I learned that fine dining required multiple silverware settings, most of them made with real silver! Asper took me to Chicago where we took in multiple museums, concerts, the aquarium, the planetarium, and more excellent dining. While we strolled the Magnificent Mile together, I started thinking that I could see myself living the kind of life that Asper offered me.

Long story short, just like Woo-ri, Asper and I married quickly and split up just as fast. And also, like Woo-ri, I admitted to myself that I may have viewed Asper as my own Daddy Long Legs. I still feel badly about my relationship with Asper. I messed up, and I accept responsibility for my part in the failed marriage. By the time I started dating Miguel, I had started reflecting on my failures with Asper so I would not repeat the same mistakes.

Right after divorcing Asper, I sped up my life. For years, I'd recommended to my clients who stayed trapped in the trauma warring in their own heads that they get lost in pleasant distraction. I took my own advice. But in my case, I chose activities that gave me hours alone to think and heal.

First, I started running, an activity that liberated my mind. Second, I learned how to cook, quite serendipitously. After receiving a free French chicken recipe in the mail, having nothing else to do or anyone else to spend time with, I decided to try it out. It tasted so delicious that I started to wonder if I should have been a chef! Third, I took charge of the house, which meant taking care of the landscaping. Up to this point, I assumed magical fairies cut the lawn, pulled the weeds, trimmed the bushes, and cleaned the pool. I soon learned that it took a team of paid magical fairies to keep my yard perfect, and the magic they used was long hours of physical labor. Asper had hired the landscapers, and he cancelled their services when he left. As I took on the role of tedious yardwork, I found a pleasant reward: space to heal. The effort I put into the yard and home served as a living amends to what I wished I could have brought to my marriage with Asper.

As I started to heal, I had an *ah-ha* moment about why things with Asper had gone so poorly. Grandiosity! Somewhere in childhood, I adopted the practice of behaving like I was superior to others to mask my low self-esteem. Grandiosity protected my self-esteem from taking blow after blow. Eventually, I believed my own lie, and I started to view my own life experiences as so unique that only a truly gifted, superior being could understand me or my feelings. So I treated Asper as though I were perfect and he carried multiple flaws, which led me to criticize him to the point of disrespect and disregard.

Growing up in South Korea, I took second place to my intellectually gifted brother, Young Suk. My parents doted on him, provided him with private lessons, and sent him to the best schools for a time. His IQ was higher than mine by seven points, but based on how differently our parents treated the two of us, I might as well have been invisible. Not once did they look over my homework or show interest in my school performance. Since my mom thought I was ugly, it didn't matter what clothes I wore, so she never bothered to buy me any. Instead, she gave me my brother's hand-me-downs that were, of course, way too big for me.

In college, when I saw other girls wearing make-up, I bought some with my own money to make myself appear prettier. When my father saw me wearing it, he forbade me from using it. So I never learned how to use make-up while in Korea. After Asper left me, I finally learned how to apply make-up to the point where I felt naked without it. I wouldn't dream of hauling the trash to the curb without at least donning foundation, eyeliner, and lipstick.

When I used my newfound skills of expertly applying emulsifiers, moisturizers, and coloring agents on my face, I felt pretty. While I hadn't yet dealt with the reason for my missing self-esteem, make-up offered me an esteem boost, if only superficially, at least enough for me to build a social life.

I shared almost every activity in my life with Asper, and so when he left, I was lost. The void I felt inside sent out an invisible yet palpable signal to those around me that I was lonely, perhaps to the point of needy.

"Heawon," one of my coworkers said to me at work, "why don't you come join me at the gym?"

"No, thank you," I said. "I don't play basketball." In my mind, a gymnasium was the place where the New York Knicks played basketball, just a big open court with nets at each end and seats around the perimeter.

"You're so funny!" she laughed, not catching on to my ignorance. "I got a couple of free passes to my gym. Bring some workout clothes with you tomorrow, and we'll go during lunch, OK?"

Walking into the gym for the first time terrified me with its rows upon rows of instruments that looked like mechanical torture devices. I felt self-conscious, as I didn't realize there were specific clothes designed for workouts. I just wore a T-shirt and shorts. Compared to other girls, I looked like I didn't belong there. While my coworker left to work out, I stared at machines I had no idea how to use. I couldn't tell if I should straddle them, chase them, or let them have their way with me.

"You look confused," a young man came up to me after a few minutes. "First time here?"

"Yes," I said self-consciously.

"Yeah, this place can feel overwhelming at first," he nodded kindly. "Why don't I give you a quick tour and show you what each machine does?"

Thank God for this man! He demystified the machinery for me, introducing me to people along the tour. The gym held its own culture, and it felt like anyone that passed through its doors became family. As I continued taking this impromptu, informal tour, I noticed a couple of men checking me out. Not in a creepy, lascivious way, but I could feel them running their eyes over me with approval.

It was an entirely new experience for me to have men who didn't know me watching this way.

Men at the gym weren't the only ones who started taking notice of me. The man at the local coffee shop often sent free coffee to me at my office, making the women I worked with envious.

"Someone's got a crush on you, Heawon!" my coworker laughed as another cup of coffee arrived for me one afternoon.

"Hush," I laughed back. "He's nice to everyone."

"He's never been 'free-coffee-nice' to me before, and I've been buying coffee from him for years!" she said with another laugh.

Shortly after that, I met Miguel through the eHarmony of the era: a personal ad in the local paper. I wasn't yet legally divorced from Asper, but I was so very lonely. What attracted me to Miguel was that he was the anti-Asper. Where Asper had been cultured, Miguel seemed strong, almost primitive. While Asper had several advanced degrees, Miguel had only an associate's degree from a community college. Instead of Asper's strong people skills, Miguel fixed complex machinery as a computer engineer. While Asper had taken me on vacations across the US, Miguel's work abroad provided me with regular international travel to intriguing cultures and lands.

Of course, being with Miguel came with a new challenge for me, specifically that work took him on the road regularly, leaving me alone in my big house. Asper and I were joined at the hip all the time. Miguel and I stay connected by long-distance phone calls.

As the reality of living alone set in, I went to the dog kennel looking for an Akita or German shepherd—any breed fierce enough to help me feel safe when Miguel traveled.

I'd been suffering from repetitive nightmares of drowning, wherein my brother would pull my legs down from his position underwater. In another dream, my brother would show up at the front door of my house.

But when I got to the kennel, a tiny golden retriever puppy greeted me and claimed me as his own. I named him Paduki after a dog in a children's book I'd read years earlier. I wanted a protector, but instead Paduki became my best friend, a creature who taught me what love looked like for the very first time. Always by my side, he offered loyalty, affection, patience, kindness, playfulness, and all the other things I didn't even know I wanted. We did everything together: walking, running, taking long drives, and even sleeping in the same bed. And with Paduki sleeping by my side, I felt protected from any who might attack me in my dreams.

I'd always wanted a dog and actually had one for a day when I was ten years old. Mom agreed to get a puppy, and I was so happy and excited. It was a brutally cold day in winter when she brought home a day-old puppy and put it outside. I begged her to take it inside, as it was below zero outside. She refused, saying it would be OK. The next morning, I found the dog outside where my mother left him, stiff and frozen to death.

I'd still cry when I thought of that little baby. Now that I no longer had my mother calling the shots in my life, I poured all of my love into Paduki. In my own way, I did this as a tribute and broken apology to the ill-fated puppy that entered my childhood home one day and my mom left outside, alone and abandoned, until he froze to death less than a day later.

Miguel's sister and her family enjoyed a Hamptons' lifestyle in a gorgeous home. Even when Miguel traveled, they invited me to join them on the weekends. I would create scrumptious dinners and host them as well. I'd always wanted a loving family, and they filled that void in me.

"We need to sell the house," Asper reminded me of my financial reality on the phone. "I can't keep paying for a home I'm not living in. You can buy me out, or we need to sell it. Either way, I need to be out from under it."

My huge home came with an equally huge mortgage, and I couldn't afford to keep up the payments on just my salary. If I wanted to stay there, I needed someone else to share the burden.

Eventually, I fell in love with Miguel and decided the two of us should be together—in my home, I hoped.

"What do you think about buying the other half of the house?" I asked Miguel one night. "You must be tired of renting a house with your brother. This way we would both have equity and own a house together."

Yeah, so instead of a marriage proposal, I made Miguel a business one, figuring if things didn't work out between us, we could always sell the house later for a profit.

"I don't know," he sighed. "I love the house, but that's a very big undertaking."

"But you'd be building equity in the house," I argued. "Renting a house is like throwing money away. Wouldn't you rather own half of something that's going to keep increasing in value over time instead of wasting money on rent? Besides, Paduki wants you to be here with us, too!"

Miguel eventually agreed. We drew up the papers. Where Asper's name had been on the mortgage, Miguel's now replaced his.

Miguel and I continued our undefined relationship like this for years. Miguel would leave the country often, and sometimes I'd join him on the road for a week here and there to go see the world. When I wasn't with him abroad, I'd spend time with Paduki, Margherita, and Miguel's family while continuing to improve my running and perfecting my chef skills.

I'd like to say that I had no problem adjusting to life with Miguel. However, that would be a lie. Like any relationship, we had our struggles. For a long while though, I denied we had any problems. I continued to do the hard work of understanding myself while keeping busy with clients, friends, cooking, running, and my sweet dog.

As I finally went to bed that evening, I thought about Socrates dictum that "an unexamined life is not worth living." As I reflected on the layers of my past, I realized that if I wanted to continue growing as a person and therapist, I had some deep self-study ahead of me.

Chapter Five

"Free expression of resentment against one's parents represents a great opportunity. It provides access to one's true self, reactivates numbed feelings, and opens that way for mourning."
—Alice Miller

Before I could examine my own life, I needed to process the family and world I'd been born into. As I ran through my neighborhood the next morning, I reflected on what I knew about my parents' history.

In 1910, Japan annexed Korea and laid claim on the Korean peninsula until the end of World War II. During those years, the Japanese Empire attempted to erase Korean culture by replacing it with their own. Nearly 100,000 Japanese families were given land in Korea, while more than 750,000 Koreans were forced into labor in Japan and other Japanese territories. Many of the enslaved were euphemistically called "comfort women" and forced into sexual slavery.

The new occupying Japanese force cut down millions of trees, replacing them with native Japanese species. One-third of Gyeongbokgung, the royal palace in Seoul built in 1395, was destroyed. As the occupation grew, the Japanese built Shinto shrines of worship. Eventually, Koreans were forced to worship the Japanese gods, including Japan's dead emperors. Forbidden from speaking Korean, Japan mandated that all Korean students be taught in Japanese.

The Japanese occupiers burned hundreds of thousands of historical Korean documents to further remove Korean people from their proud heritage. Eventually, the Japanese forced Koreans to assume Japanese surnames. Those who refused didn't receive mail or ration cards and ceased to exist in the eyes of the occupiers.

My mother's and father's early years were spent in the turmoil, hardships, and sadness of the Japanese occupation.

"Come quickly!" a friend of my grandfather's shouted excitedly to him as he pulled his small fishing boat out of the water. "You're a father!"

"Again?" Grandpa said with a shrug.

"Yes," his friend laughed. "Is this your eleventh child?"

"Twelfth, I think," Grandpa replied with another shrug. "Well, I guess I should go see my baby. Can you take care of my catch?"

"Of course. Now go!"

"Ah, it is a boy, yes?" Grandpa asked, showing curiosity for the first time.

"Yes, you have another son."

Living in a primitive mud hut outside of Busan, South Korea, just a few feet from the China Sea, Grandpa went to see his newest child. When he saw his small boy in his wife's arms, Grandpa allowed himself a smile.

"We shall call him Mandoo," Grandpa announced.

Koreans of that time often gave their children intentionally awful names, believing that bad names promoted longevity. *Mandoo* means dumpling, and Grandpa named my father Dumpling as a sign of love and a wish for my father's long life. As hard as it must have been for my father to grow up named Dumpling, he likely had an easier time than his brothers, Cow Head, Horse Head, and some with even worse names.

Born in 1933, father was the last of twelve children in his family. As poor as they were, they ate well, having their pick from the freshest bounty of the China Sea. Grandpa, like most of those living on the water's edge, worked as a fisherman. The plan for Dad's future was to join his father and brothers as a fisherman, but the Korean War altered his trajectory.

Near the end of WWII, Japan sought assistance from the Soviet Union, which brought the Communists into the Korean Peninsula. In response, the United States intervened in an attempt to prevent the Peninsula from uniting as a Soviet satellite state.

Starting in 1950 and lasting for more than three years, the Korean War claimed more than three million lives, most of them Korean civilians. Blood literally filled the streets of Seoul, as the city was captured and recaptured several times.

When the US Navy arrived at the Busan port as the Korean conflict began, my father, then a teenager, found a new direction for his life.

"You there!" a sailor yelled at my dad who stood at the port watching the ships. "You don't by any chance happen to speak English, do ya?"

Dad knew the word *English,* and shook his head *no.*

"Nuts," the sailor said. After thinking for a moment, the sailor motioned my father to come closer. Then he ripped off a piece of paper with an address written on it and handed it to my dad.

"Do you know where this is?" he asked.

Although Dad didn't know what the man asked him, his eyes lit up when he recognized the address.

"*Iri, iri*!" my father said, motioning for the sailor to follow him.

"Okay, so you know where this is? Great! Let's go!" the sailor said, walking next to my dad.

From that day on, my dad became a go-fer for the US military personnel stationed in the area. He stayed close to the US sailors, running errands several times each day, earning a reputation for someone with smarts and eagerness while also getting a few dollars for his efforts. The sailors taught my dad English, a language he picked up quickly.

When the US military needed help getting supplies and food rations to the Korean people, my dad worked alongside them. Korea had no infrastructure for social services at the time. In fact, the concept of social work was brand new in Korea, and my father loved every aspect of it.

Given his usefulness to the efforts of the US forces, Dad soon found work with the Canadian Unitarian Welfare Society, a role that afforded him perks like choice clothes and food as well as instruction on the ins and outs of social support and charity. Dad felt deeply honored to help his fellow Koreans.

By 1954, thanks to his growing fluency in English and frontline exposure to social work, my dad got accepted into college in Seoul where he joined the first generation of students studying social work.

While earning his degree in social work, he met my mother, a pretty, young woman and fellow social work student named Pak Soon Ryul who was three years older than him.

While my father spent his early years at the China Sea, my mother came from the Dague region, a mountainous area of Korea, but the two shared the common bond of growing up in great poverty.

My mom's house, like my father's, was nothing but a grass and mud hut. But the house didn't protect her from the evils within those walls. When Mom was seven, her older brother and some male cousins sexually molested her during the night. To escape their abuse, she slept outside in the open, willingly accepting the possibility of being attacked by wild animals if it meant escaping the human animals that hurt her inside of her hut.

A year later in 1938, the Japanese colonialists sent my mom to Japan to work as a slave for a family there. She never talked about her time in captivity in Japan other than that the master of the house was nice. She remained a captive until 1945 when the War in the Pacific ended.

To welcome my mom home, her own mother prepared all of Mom's favorite foods. Each time my mother told me this story, which was often, she skipped over the brutal details about her slavery in Japan. Instead, she glowed—remembering how wonderful her mother had been to remember her and make her traditional Korean foods once she returned. She never shared any other details about her mom to justify why she was considered such a wonderful mother—giving me serious doubt about the reality of this.

Knowing about the sexual abuse she suffered at the hands of her brother and cousins, I always wondered why my grandmother didn't intervene. Had my mom told her about it? If not, why not? Something didn't add up, but according to my mom, my grandmother was a saint.

Mother's peaceful reunification with her family after the War didn't last long. By the time the Korean War began in 1950, my then twenty-year-old mother found herself walking in the middle of Seoul where the falling rain mixed with the blood of countless civilians slain in the streets. She spoke of this time once and then never mentioned it again.

My mother blocked out her early life trauma, choosing to detach from it as if it happened to someone else. Instead of talking about her grief or anger, she bottled it up—until something from her past trauma triggered her. Then, she would lash out. Usually though, she internalized her pain and twisted it until it fomented into what I later learned was a narcissistic personality.

Somehow, she fought back against her poverty and trauma, and she gained acceptance in Kangnam Social Welfare University, where she entered the social work program. While she lacked the ability to confront her own traumas, she loved the idea of improving others' lives. Maybe the thought of helping others put her in a position of power over them. Whatever drove her to study social work, her schooling afforded her the opportunity to meet my father, who studied social work in the same school. After the two met, they grew inseparable.

After getting married, both my father and mother served as social workers—Dad more so than my mom. Dad was always driven, and he never stopped learning and working. Starting as a medical social worker, he then took a job with the Canada Unitarian Society, the Mokpo Child Hospital, and Inchon Social Welfare Agency. In 1975, he completed his master's program in social work in Japan, and then served as a professor at Kangnam Social Welfare University—and Ewha University, the top female-only university in South Korea.

Along the way, he wrote and published books and articles on social work while also translating well-known works into Korean. The seminal research papers he wrote on social welfare policy and law still serve as the foundation for many aspects of South Korean society today. He assisted Korean Congress to develop the National Health Insurance where everyone in the country received healthcare.

For several years, he served as the president of the Korean Association of Social Workers. He finally retired from teaching in 1999, leaving a legacy in the thousands of students he taught and the millions of South Koreans' lives that he touched. Even though my father wasn't a therapist or psychoanalyst, he introduced Western psychiatry and social services to the East. At the time, authorities in the field of social work called him, "Korean Freud." That made me the "Daughter of Korean Freud."

For her part, Mom continued in social work until 1959 when she received wonderful news from the midwife.

"Congratulations," the midwife confirmed. "You are expecting a child!"

As soon as she learned she carried a child, she quit working and started creating a home to introduce their baby.

In 1960, Mom and Dad welcomed my brother, Young Suk, into their world. Their family grew three years later when my mom learned she was pregnant again. I entered the world in June of 1963.

For most Korean couples, having a son first followed by a daughter would bring contentment and joy to the household. But despite Dad's growing success in his career and financial condition as well the family now having two healthy children, Mom continued to slip into her own world. She never showed any interest in my schoolwork. And I never saw her cleaning the house. In fact, I grew up thinking that every household replaced their floors when they got dirty rather than clean them. It wasn't until Asper told me about mopping and I read a book on cleaning that I understood the concept!

But cleaning wasn't the extent of her or my family's problems. Whenever a fellow student in my social work classes asked what it was like to be the daughter of the famous Korean Freud, I'd cringe inside. While many envied me for having such a renowned dad, I would have to fight the urge to scream in despair about the pain my family caused me.

By the time I completed my run, I acknowledged that my parents endured unspeakable traumas in their lives. I also recognized that I'd entered a world where my mother's detachment and manipulation became normal to me. As a result, I, too, embraced emotional detachment at times when I felt the need to protect myself.

These memories began tickling a part of me that I knew needed more investigation. I'd seen in my clients how ignoring such experiences could create holes or dysfunction in their lives. *I have a lot of work to do, and I'm going to do it,* I committed as I left for work that morning.

Chapter Six

"The wounded recognized the wounded."
—Nora Roberts, *Rising Tides*

By the time Thursday afternoon came around, I couldn't wait to see Woo-ri. She'd left abruptly at the conclusion of our previous session, and her recurring nightmare about the earthquake on her honeymoon might have roots in her childhood.

From what I'd heard of Woo-ri's story, she and I had many things in common. The more time I spent with her, the more my own past traumas roiled within me.

"Hello Woo-ri," I said warmly as she swept into my office and found her now familiar place on my sofa.

"Hello," she greeted me warmly. "Did you miss me?" she added playfully.

"Oh, *Mani!*" I replied in the same spirit, telling her that I missed her very much indeed.

We both laughed for a moment as we settled into our spots and got comfortable.

"If it's OK with you, I'd like to pick up where we left off last time," I got started. "Is that alright?"

"That's fine," she said, pulling her legs up under her on the couch.

"I know your marriage didn't last, but I'd like to hear more about what happened when you returned from your honeymoon," I launched in, deciding not to probe her any further about her brother so early in our meetings.

"OK," she nodded. "I told you when we got back from our honeymoon that everyone joked saying we started off on 'shaky ground.' While they were joking, I took their words to heart. But then we found a dream house outside the city. It came with a huge price, like my five-hour commute to and from work. This reminded me of the commute I had in the high school I attended in South Korea, which started at 8:00 a.m. for students with high grades. Other students started their class at 9:00. To get to school on time, I had to leave home by 5:30 a.m. Of course, when it rained or snowed, I had to leave even earlier. Since I also attended a special academy in Seoul for extra help after school, I didn't get home until 11:00 p.m. Between homework and studying, I hardly slept."

"I don't understand. Why did you attend a school that was so far away?"

Woo-ri was quiet for a little while and then explained it to me. "The principal at my high school knew my dad. Since his school had the lowest college admission rates in the region, and since I had good grades, the principal asked my dad to keep me there even after my family moved hours away. So my dad promised to the principal that he would not transfer me to a school closer to where we lived. I felt like my dad academically pimped me out!"

I took time to digest her story, but I knew that whatever term Woo-ri wanted to assign to her father's actions, "pimping her out" fit. *Having to commute five or more hours a day for three years just because her dad wanted to look good to the principal?* I thought. I recalled how stressed out I'd been in high school when preparing for college admission in South Korea. I could hardly imagine that during the most important years of Woo-ri's schooling that her dad made a decision that nearly sabotaged his own daughter's success.

"Did I mention I worked six days a week?" Woo-ri said, bringing me back to the session. "My husband had it easy compared to me," she added, reminding me of our original discussion. "Thirty hours commuting and fifty hours working. If I wanted that for my life, I could have stayed in South Korea. I always thought if you worked hard, got a good education, found a job you enjoyed, and married well, you could build a happy future."

She paused, drifting off in thought before she continued.

"But even as things were going well, I was unhappy. I started to resent my husband. He came from a wealthy family, had a great education, and had a reasonable commute. He could have taken a job anywhere to make more money if he wanted. But instead, he kept talking about quitting so he could become an actor, right? So I found myself getting frustrated with him for having no ambition. Then one weekend, we went to a bar mitzvah for his boss's son," Woo-ri continued as I listened. "Since I didn't know many people, I liked meeting new people who might become my friends. We went, and everything seemed fine. Then later at home, we played this card game my husband taught me. But this time when we played, he kept losing. Each time he lost, he would throw his cards down hard on the table and mutter to himself."

"'What's wrong?' I asked. 'Why are you so angry? It's just a game.' Well, then he blew up at me. 'I hate this. I'm not playing anymore!' he screamed and cursed. Then he swept all the cards off the table, like he was a child having a tantrum. I hated whenever he cursed, even though his curses weren't directed at me. You know how it is in Korea. We think people who curse are worse than the worst. I got turned off completely after the first time I heard him use a curse word.

"I didn't know what to say to him, so I left and went into our bedroom and closed the door," Woo-ri continued. "He ran to the bedroom after me. And he pushed the bedroom door open with so much force that he smashed a hole in the wall. You know, from the doorknob. 'The boss gave me a huge job, and I did amazing work on it,'" he screamed at me. 'But at the party, did my boss thank me or tell me that I did a good job? No! Do you know what he talked about instead? How beautiful my wife is! How do you think that makes me feel?'"

"His anger that came out when you played cards was misplaced jealously?" I asked, trying to follow the story.

"I guess," Woo-ri shrugged. "But I hardly even talked to his boss. This wasn't my party. I only went because of my husband. Should I have ignored his boss? So now, my husband is maybe jealous because of the attention his boss paid to me."

"How often did this sort of thing happen? Your husband getting jealous, I mean?" I asked.

"Not often," Woo-ri answered. "Do you know what I think? My husband liked me being a helpless and needy woman with few friends. That way, he could feel good about himself because he got to rescue me. But when I started to feel more comfortable, he became a different person. He needed to be a hero—to me, to his boss, to his family, to everyone. And when he wasn't treated like a hero, he got moody, even angry."

"That's a very astute observation," I said, writing something in my notebook.

"When we first met, we were so nice and kind to each other. And we were tender, even if I felt no romantic spark. Maybe *gentle* is a better word than tender. But as time passed, we kept blowing up at each other. I didn't like who we were becoming as people. Or as a couple," Woo-ri added.

"What did you do when your husband came in screaming at you?" I asked, leaning forward, eager to hear the rest of her story.

"At a young age, I decided that I'd never again allow a person to abuse me," Woo-ri spoke quickly.

She said "again," which confirmed my suspicion. And she used the word "abuse," I noted. I need to explore this later, I noted to myself.

"I had a male cousin who beat up his sister one day," Woo-ri continued sharing. "My aunt told my mother that her daughter stopped her brother from abusing her by tearing apart the family room. She knocked things off the wall, smashed some ceramic figurines, and screamed like a crazy person. Her brother never touched her again. He was afraid of her because she showed him her rage. So that's what I did! I thought if I acted like my cousin, I could stop my husband from acting violently. I went into the kitchen and started smashing glasses on the floor. Glass flew everywhere."

I could see Woo-ri's face tense as she relived this memory. She looked me in the eyes as she continued.

"Then my husband ran into the dining room. I watched as he pulled our wedding pictures off the wall. And then he smashed them on the floor and stomped on them," Woo-ri reported the scene that replayed in her mind. "But when *he* started breaking things, I didn't feel safe. Things were getting out of control. Even when I was breaking glasses, I felt scared inside. I'd never acted like this before."

"What did you do?"

"I called 911," she answered immediately. "I didn't know what else to do! And they, the police, came out quickly. I told them what happened and asked them to help stop the violence."

"'Okay,' one of the men said to me, 'You should leave the house.'

"'How can I leave the house? I have nowhere to go. My husband has family nearby, so he should leave.' I told them. So the policeman asks him to leave. My husband put some things in a bag, and he left."

"Did that end the crisis for the night?" I asked.

"Yes, but then I had a new crisis. I didn't know what to do

afterwards," Woo-ri answered. "I'd never done anything like that before. But when I got scared, remembering what my aunt told me, I thought I could make my husband calm down if I acted crazier than him. I would have done anything to keep him from abusing me. But then I didn't know what to do next."

"Where did he go?" I asked.

"He stayed with his younger brother. Then he went to his parents' house, and he told them everything that happened. I still felt terrible about that night, and I could only imagine what his family must have thought of me. He didn't call me, and I didn't call him. I thought we both needed time to cool down," Woo-ri shrugged, "since we had both acted like children the last time we saw one another."

"How long did you two go without speaking?" I asked.

"A week," she answered. "Then I thought that this was silly. We should talk like adults. I called him and asked him to meet me at a restaurant so we could make peace."

"I showed up first and sat at the bar," Woo-ri said, her eyes looking into the past. "A man at the bar started talking with me just as my husband walked in. As soon as my husband sees me talking with another man, his face gets cloudy as if he were thinking, 'There she goes again.'

Once we sat down together, he started talking about what happened that Sunday night when we both lost control. I reminded him that he made a big hole in the wall from the doorknob. He didn't remember doing that. But he remembered what I did next, and that's what he wanted to talk about.

"'No,'" I told him. "'That's not what happened. It started when we were playing cards. You got angry and said you weren't going to play anymore. Then I left to go into the bedroom.' I told him everything that had happened that night. Finally, he admitted his part."

"Then what happened?"

"'That's it,' he said. 'We're done.' That's what he said. And then I didn't know what to say," Woo-ri shook her head. "I'd met him to reconcile. We'd both been childish, but I never imagined that he'd leave because of this."

"Did you tell him that?" I asked.

"I did," Woo-ri said quickly. "I told him that we could work through this."

"What did he say?"

"He wanted a divorce," Woo-ri stated with a far-off stare. "He told me that he'd never behaved that way before in his life, and it scared him. He didn't want to risk ever acting that way again. Also, he could lose his license as a lawyer if he were convicted for domestic violence."

"What went through your mind when he said that?"

"We hadn't been married a year. I didn't know what was going to happen to me."

"What do you mean?" I asked to make sure I understood her feelings.

"I didn't know what my life would look like after him," she said, choosing her words carefully. "I wanted to reconcile, because I didn't want to face the unknown. I knew him. I knew life with him. We weren't very happy, and we didn't seem to move in the same direction. But our life together had been mostly predictable. I never thought about what my life would look like if I were alone. It scared me. But at the same time, I know I didn't love him like a wife should love her husband. He deserved better. I liked him as friend, especially when I was helpless, and he rode up on a white horse to save me. I wish I could have loved him. I had no idea what the future held, but I knew that it was probably the right thing to do."

"So you divorced?" I asked as a statement.

"Yes," Woo-ri sighed. "He took care of everything, since he was a lawyer. All I had to do was sign some papers. I never got to say goodbye to his family. I didn't know that Sunday night when things got out of hand that we would never live as husband and wife again. It's sad."

"Why do you think you started having the recurring nightmare about the earthquake on your honeymoon so many years later?" I asked, trying to get her to pinpoint any triggering events in her life. "Do you feel unsafe again?"

"Hmm," Woo-ri vocalized in response.

I waited for her to process her thoughts.

"I haven't had that nightmare since I've started coming to see you," Woo-ri said, dodging my question.

"Do you think talking about it has removed it from your subconscious to your conscious thoughts, so it doesn't plague your dreams?" I wondered.

"I don't know," she shrugged. "Other nightmares have taken its place," Woo-ri said, shifting in her seat.

"Can you tell me about those nightmares?" I asked, wondering if she might reveal a clue to what troubled her.

"I'm a child back in South Korea," she started. "My brother and I walk in the mountains in Seoul. He leads me by the hand to a cliff, and we stand on a ledge over a lake." Woo-ri's face tensed, and I'm sure my own face went white.

"Then he's no longer standing beside me. He's behind me. Instead of holding my hand, he puts his hands on my shoulders. I'm scared, because I don't know what he's going to do. I start crying and begging him not to push me," Woo-ri said, suddenly aware that she's crying as she speaks.

"Then what happens?" I ask, feeling sick, and not just for the plight she faced in her dream.

"Nothing," she sniffs quickly and wipes her eyes. "Nothing happens. That's when I wake up."

"Is this like your nightmare of the earthquake where you dream about the events that actually happened to you?" I pushed.

"No," she said, closing the conversation. "It's just a stupid dream."

"It sounds terrifying," I told her, my own chest beating hard and voice shaking as I spoke. "I'm glad that it was only a dream."

"I have to go," Woo-ri said, standing up suddenly. "Today was good. Thank you. I will see you next Thursday," she said as she slipped out of my office and softly closed the door behind her.

"Dear God, my child," I spoke after she closed the door. "What hell did you live through?" I felt tears well up in my eyes, and I needed several moments to collect myself before leaving my office for the day.

Chapter Seven

"Family is supposed to be our safe haven. Very often, it's the place where we find the deepest heartache."
—Iyanla Vanzant

"How was your meeting with Woo-ri today?" Margherita asked me over dinner.

I'd called Margherita telling her that I'd be late. After work, I returned home to let my dog out and took a shower to wash the day off of myself.

"I'm still processing everything," I told her honestly. "She shared more details about her marriage and divorce. I'm starting to really understand her."

Margherita nodded. "Well, you're both Korean-born women and close in age. Does she remind you of yourself?"

I didn't want to answer. If I told her the truth, I worried that I would be exposing parts of myself that I didn't like, couldn't accept, and had been working to change.

Yet, Margherita knew me better than anyone else. I owed her some sort of answer.

"Well," I started speaking, thinking through my words carefully, "Woo-ri is focused, hard-working, and driven. She expects a lot for herself, and she expected a lot from her husband, which is part of why her marriage failed."

"Does she display grandiosity?" Margherita asked.

"I'm not sure I would go that far," I said quickly, more in defense of my awareness of my own struggles than to help Woo-ri save face. "I think it's common to expect those closest to us to reciprocate our own energy and spirit. Americans grow up living the American Dream, so many of them don't see that dream as special. But when you're born in another country and move here, you expect to see Americans actively pursuing that dream. I think that's why Woo-ri believed her husband wasn't as hungry to succeed as she was. He took his American privilege for granted."

"Did you ever feel that way when you were married to Asper?" Margherita asked, her love for me as a friend melding into the questions she might ask as my therapist.

"Maybe a little," I said with a shrug. "I worked hard in college and graduate school. Asper never had to work as hard as I did. So that's a part of it. But I also moved from one country to another and had to learn a new language at the same time. I didn't blame Asper for not understanding how hard I pushed myself to make something of myself, but my struggles weren't something he could relate to."

"Like what?" she asked.

"Like speaking English," I said quickly. "The letter 'a' doesn't make one sound. It makes nine different ones! When you're born in America, you just learn to read, write, and speak English, because you're exposed to it from birth. But being from South Korea, even after many years of studying English, I had to translate nearly every word in my head before I could speak aloud. And it's still hard for me sometimes."

"That makes sense," Margherita nodded.

After thinking a few moments, I thought of an even more powerful example to share with her.

"Maybe I can share a better example with you about how helpless I felt not speaking English fluently," I said. "When I got to Adelphi University housing, it was closed for construction. I went to international studies. Its director, Edith Calhoun, found a Korean student to translate for me, since I couldn't explain my situation clearly in English. The student brought me a Korean newspaper that had a rental section. We found a Korean female who was looking for a roommate to share a studio in Queens. Dr. Calhoun told me that housing wouldn't be available on campus for me until September, so I needed to find a place for two months. Can you imagine how lost I felt? I don't even want to think about what might have happened if I hadn't found Dr. Calhoun and a Korean student to help me translate. I might still be sleeping in an alley!" I joked.

"Wow," Margherita sighed. "No, I can't imagine that either."

"Well, it turned out that my roommate was a student in the master's program for theology, which made me very happy to live with a fellow Christian. After I moved in, I started exploring the neighborhood and NYC. Then one afternoon, I returned to the apartment, and my roommate came at me with a knife, screaming that she knew I'd been listening in on her phone conversations! I didn't know it at the time, but she suffered from schizophrenic paranoia. So what did I do? I didn't know how to call the police, and even if I could, I didn't speak enough English to tell them what was happening. I had no place to go."

"Oh, Heawon," Margherita said, her face full of empathy.

"So I ran back outside and started checking at the local churches to see if they would let me stay overnight just until I could figure something out. That's when I learned that US churches are different than those in Korea. In Korea, churches are open during the night so that people can come in and pray. But here, I could find no church open. I had no choice but to return to the apartment. But since I was too afraid to go back into my unit, I found that the boiler room in our building wasn't locked. I slept on the floor of the boiler room for two months. And I'm being very literal when I say that the boiler room was over a hundred degrees, and I had to swat rats off me each night when they'd come out and try to eat my face and body. But what else could I do?"

By the time I finished my story, Margherita had her hands on either side of her face and tears in her eyes.

"Anyway," I concluded, "I'm sorry for sharing this with you. But I wanted you to see how hard things are for people like me and Woo-ri who leave a world we know to enter one where we know nothing. I didn't blame Asper for not understanding how hard I found it to do things that came easily to him, but I don't think he related to my struggles."

"Well, I will never see the challenges of people coming to the US the same way again," Margherita said after a long sigh.

I felt good with my answer. I didn't need to expose my own grandiosity and emotional detachment in how I behaved in my marriage. Nor did I want to share my mother's narcissistic personality or the trauma of my childhood.

"Anyway," I changed the subject, "Woo-ri told me that she hasn't had her earthquake nightmare since she started seeing me. That's good."

"Sometimes sharing our thoughts and fears keeps them from tormenting our subconscious when we're sleeping," she nodded, her face still wearing the heaviness of my story.

"That's what I told her," I agreed. "But she shared another nightmare she's having—one where her brother threatens to push her off a cliff into a lake. While she didn't cry when she told me about the earthquake, she became quite emotional when she shared the dream about her brother. She also indicated she was abused in the past."

"Well, you figured her brother had abused her somehow," Margherita answered before adding, "and it sounds like you were right."

"In some ways, I feel like I'm still just scratching the surface on her trauma," I responded. "But little by little, she's sharing more."

"If anyone can break through to her, my friend, it's you," Margherita said while tenderly squeezing my hand.

When I got home that night, I changed into my pajamas, poured myself a glass of wine, lowered the lights in the living room, cuddled with Paduki, and let out a long, exhausted sigh.

Speaking Korean with Woo-ri switched on my Korean brain. The debrief I had with Margherita left me even more raw, as she forced me to confront memories of my past. I felt raw as childhood memories resurfaced and ripped at my heart.

I sat on the floor, leaning back against the couch, imagining I could see Woo-ri at the mountain's edge. I pictured the scene: Woo-ri as a small child, teetering on the cliff, her faceless, nameless brother looming over her. And then Woo-ri's sweet face morphed into mine, and her brother transformed into Young Suk. My eyes grew wide as I felt his rough hands on my shoulders, his seemingly dead eyes looking through me. I cried, but no one could hear me. My squirms heightened his pleasure, and he smiled as I twisted to get free.

Suddenly, I felt a rock strike my head in an explosion of light and red. Blood, my own, dripped through my fingers. The next thing I knew, I was flying through the air, and I hit the deep, cold water. My world grew dark. When I awoke, thorns and brambles cut deeply into my flesh, opening both old and new wounds. Then I flew again, this time crashing into a bedroom wall before fists and feet pummeled me as I wrapped my arms and hands around my head.

"HOW COULD YOU DO THIS TO ME?" a detached, hellish growl shot out of my mouth.

I sat sobbing on the floor with my arms wrapped around myself like a bear hug as I rocked back and forth. At some point, I felt Paduki's legs on my shoulders and his tongue against my cheeks as he tasted my tears. Then Paduki let out a whine. I believe that his heart hurt to see me in such pain, and a new gush of tears fell as I held onto my loving dog like he was a life preserver.

My mind went back several years to the first time I feared my brother, Young Suk.

"Brother," seven-year-old me sang out to my brother in my little girl sing-songy voice, "Mom said we should walk home together."

This had been our first day of attending the same school together. While my brother had gone to an elite private school before, for some reason he stopped going there and started coming to my public school. That made me happy. I wouldn't have to walk those thirty minutes to and from school alone, something scary for a seven-year-old, especially when kidnapping was rampant. I knew that children had been taken from this path and never seen again.

Instead of answering me, he kicked a rock down the road in front of him. As I waited for him to catch up to me, I looked around for any signs of danger.

Smack! My head exploded in pain as something hard smacked against my skull from behind. I screamed and put my hand to my head. When I brought my hand back down, I saw blood running through my fingers. Immediately I looked for my brother to come help me, and I couldn't understand why he wasn't rushing to my side.

Then I turned and saw him, ten feet away, with his hands on his hips and emptiness in his eyes as he looked through me. I felt confused at first, and then terrified. When I stepped back from the path, I saw a large rock on the ground next to me. *Young Suk wasn't helping me because he was the one who'd hurt me*, I finally realized. He'd thrown the rock. Once he drew blood, he'd stood back to watch me suffer.

Up until this moment, I'd always loved my brother. We'd played together for years, exploring the many mountains and trails with our shared friends. When he started school, I looked out the window, waiting for his return like a puppy longing for the return of its master.

Everything I wanted to believe about my brother and family's love collapsed in that moment. I cried, both for my physical pain and in terror of what he might do to me in the future.

Finally, Young Suk started to move over to where I stood crying. As he approached, I put my hands over my head and flinched. In the back of my mind though, I hoped he'd thrown the rock at me for the same reason young boys throw rocks at birds: they never expect to hit them. *He'll see the pain he caused me, and then he'll apologize and comfort me,* I wanted to believe.

"Heawon," he said, grabbing my face roughly in his hands so I could see the darkness in his eyes, "if you say anything to Mom and Dad, I will kill you. Do you understand?"

It would have been easier for me had he killed me in that moment. The terror he put in me through by his actions and words, without provocation, ended my childhood forever.

"I won't tell," I managed to say between quiet sobs.

When I got home, I couldn't hide the blood on my head, hands, and clothes.

"What did you do?" my mother asked with annoyance.

Young Suk glared at me from behind my mother.

"I," looking for the words to protect my brother, "I fell."

"Well, you ruined your clothes," my mother sighed in frustration. "Go wash up and change."

I never told my parents, but I kept my distance from Young Suk.

After Dad got a better job, we moved to a new area with many other young children. After school, my friends and I would visit the playground or play games in the nearby mountains. Sometimes my brother would come too, but I stayed away from him.

One afternoon while several of us played hide-and-go-seek in the mountains, I found a great hiding place in a rock crevasse on a ledge overlooking a mountain lake. I looked around to make sure no one could see my hiding place, and I backed into the small opening that concealed my little frame.

They'll never find me here! I thought with giddiness.

A few times I heard footfalls nearby, but each time the steps quickly retreated.

I have to remember this place, I told myself, pleased with my hiding spot.

Then I heard more footsteps approaching. I pushed my body as tightly as I could against the rock behind me, shut my eyes, and held my breath, wishing the seeker away.

"There you are," a voice said, forcing me to open my eyes.

It was Young Suk.

"You should go swimming," he said, his voice flat and dead-sounding.

Reaching inside my hiding place, he grabbed me by my shirt and pulled me to my feet. Then before I could get my balance, he flung me over the edge of the cliff.

"Ahhhhhhhhhhh!" I screamed and twisted through the air like an airplane with a missing wing. My little body plunged thirty feet into the icy lake below. Even before I hit the water, my mind shut down. Ice entered my veins, and my numb body sunk into the deep mountain pool.

Adults who were in the lake carried me back to my house. I must have been in and out of consciousness along the way back home, because I remember flashes of them talking quickly in worried voices.

"Heawon fell in a lake!" Young Suk told my mother as they brought me inside the house.

Shivering and disoriented, I said nothing as my mother berated me.

"Clumsy girl," she tsk-tsked me.

I didn't need my brother to remind me to say nothing of this to my parents. I never played in the mountains with my friends again.

As much as I tried to keep away from my brother, he would appear when I didn't expect to see him. I struggled to sleep at night, scared that he would come to my room and cut me...or worse.

Months later, Young Suk shoved me into a large hole in the nearby mountain where they stacked thorny branches before burning them. The size of the hole was about twenty-five by twenty-five feet. Each time I tried to move, the thorns dug into my skin, shooting pain throughout my body. That sunny summer afternoon, the sun burned especially hot. Since I couldn't move to get out of the hole—and with Young Suk standing by to make sure I didn't get out—I thought to myself, *This is how I'm going to die. Night will fall, and the workers will start burning all these branches without knowing I'm in here.*

Those thoughts echoed in my mind as I fell asleep. Then I was awakened when something hit my face. Opening my eyes, I saw Young Suk standing over the hole, throwing little pebbles at me to wake me up. Once he grew bored of me, he tossed a long stick into the pit, which I grabbed ahold of and climbed up straight out of the hole.

Although he was the one who pushed me in, I was grateful that he got me out.

"Thank you, Young Suk," I stammered.

Twisted emotions filled me, and I wanted to live and die simultaneously. I hated my brother with my entire being, yet I felt grateful that he rescued me from the pit he'd thrown me into.

"You must be more careful," my mother scolded me when I got home that afternoon, telling her that I'd fallen into the rose bushes in our front yard. While she pulled hundreds of thorns from my body, tears rolled down my face. My mother knew that I couldn't have gotten all of these thorns puncturing my body just from the three small rose bushes in front of our house. Yet Mother was complicit in keeping the secret with my brother. My heart broke.

"Yes, Mother," I said weakly.

During those years, I tried to move through the home silently, suppressing even my breathing, for fear that Young Suk would find me and hurt me. I desperately yearned for my mom's love and protection. It never came. Mom told me later that it was amazing that my body continued to develop even during those years of living like a ghost and eating next to nothing. Even she knew how terrified I felt, yet she did nothing.

My salvation came from reading biographies of famous people like Helen Keller. Blind and unable to hear before she reached two-years-old, Keller could have lived in her head and been excused for not learning. Yet Anne Sullivan, her first teacher, took time to teach her to both read and write. I read about how much patience, kindness, and love Sullivan poured into Helen Keller. Oh, how I yearned for Anne Sullivan to be my guide. So I imagined Sullivan was with me in my dark alleys, encouraging and loving me. Somehow, my childlike innocence and way of visualizing Sullivan as my own protector saved me repeatedly.

Young Suk continued to abuse me psychologically and physically throughout grade school, high school, and college. I'd eventually gone to my parents to ask them to get help for him.

"He needs to see a counselor," I begged my parents. "He needs to be on medication. He is not right. I know he's been thrown out of several schools," I told them. "And I know he's been accused of hurting a girl in town. Please get help for him before he kills someone!" I pleaded, in the back of my mind worrying that I might be that person he killed.

"Your brother is fine," my father insisted. "Any problems he's had are in the past. I won't hear another word about it," he added, effectively ending the conversation.

I talked to my parents several times about Young Suk, telling them some of the ways he hurt me. Before my father planned to go to Japan for two years to start his master of social work program, I talked to him again, this time pleading with him to stay in South Korea.

"Please, Father," I begged. "He's hurt me many times. If you leave, I'm afraid that he will finally kill me."

My parents exchanged looks. Finally, my father said, "I will discuss this with your mother."

I don't know if they ever talked about it, but my father never got back to me. Instead, he left for Japan as planned. And as soon as he left, my brother tormented me even more, just as I'd feared.

My father may have been the Korean Freud, but he had no idea how to care for his family's emotional needs. And he didn't seem to try to create a safe environment for me during all the years I lived at home. All of his accolades came from serving the country, educating graduate students, and translating the top psychological textbooks into Korean. But when it came to loving the people in his own household, he looked away.

An article written about my father stated that he worked tirelessly to serve abused and troubled kids and their families. His success came not only from the knowledge of social work, but also from the person who he was.

The person who wrote the paper obviously knew nothing of his personal life at home.

I finally got a brief respite from Young Suk when he entered compulsory military service. It didn't last long enough for my liking. Once he completed his military duty, he returned home a month before I began my final year at the university—and just weeks before I broke off my relationship with Chang.

On the day when I broke up with Chang, I came out of my room only to use the restroom. I didn't know if one could die from a broken heart, but I believed I might. The thought of food made my already-knotted stomach lurch. I had to force my lungs to let in air.

Meanwhile, my mother hummed happy songs around the house, as her joyful spirit had been renewed by my brokenness. "Dinner!" she announced loudly enough for all members of the household to hear.

To show respect for her preparing the meal, I came out of my room and told her, "I cannot eat, but thank you for making dinner," before returning to my room.

A short time later, my father and brother sat at the table as my mother started serving dinner.

"Where's Heawon?" my brother asked with contempt. "Why isn't she at the dinner table?"

I didn't hear any response from my mother or father. Seconds later, my door flew open, and Young Suk entered my room.

"Who do you think you are?" he spat out with disgust.

I sat up, confused, my mind working in slow motion, as Young Suk pulled me out of my bedding by my hair.

"Are you so *special*?" he yelled sarcastically before beating me for twenty minutes. After grabbing me by the hair, he slapped me to the ground and then kicked me as I tried to protect my head. He stopped kicking briefly before he pulled me to my feet. Then he slammed his fist into my face, knocking me back several feet.

Fortunately, I blacked out. I regained consciousness briefly as he lifted me over his head like a barbell, and then my world went dark again as he threw me into my bedroom wall.

Young Suk had just left the military. Always big and strong, he'd returned at peak strength and with specialized training in how to disable an enemy combatant. I didn't fight back. Instead, I tried to protect my skull from being fractured by his blows. He tossed me around and beat me as if I were a stuffed animal and he a vicious dog.

By the time I regained consciousness, I had cuts and bruises across my face and body. Each breath caused pain in my ribs and chest. Both legs throbbed. My left eye had swollen closed, and I wore two black eyes. Blood spilled from cuts on my lips where his knuckles had pummeled my flesh against my teeth.

My parents must have heard every scream I made, yet they did nothing. As Young Suk landed blow after blow against my tiny frame, my parents would have heard loud pops and slaps. Yet they never lifted a hand or a voice to save me.

Because of my mother, I'd just said goodbye to my first and deepest love. Instead of being met with familial compassion or love, my parents did nothing to comfort my frozen soul. And they did nothing as my brother brutally beat me while they sat twelve feet away at the dinner table.

In more anguish than I knew a person could endure, I wanted my suffering to stop. I no longer dreamed of being seen, cared for, or loved. I only wanted to escape.

I will die if I stay in South Korea, I realized again. *Maybe death is better.*

By the time I'd relived those memories, I'd rung every endorphin out of my body. Even Paduki looked spent, having remained on high alert along with my emotions all evening. I didn't think I'd be able to sleep that night, but I fell into deep slumber before turning out the light.

I expected to see bruises and abrasions across my face when I looked in the mirror the next morning, and it disappointed me that my face didn't have a mark on it. I wished I could wear my scars on the outside where they would eventually heal.

Chapter Eight

"Only to the extent that we expose ourselves over and over to annihilation can that which is indestructible in us be found. Things falling apart is not a test to overcome and solve. The truth is, things don't really get solved. They come together and then fall apart again. It's just like that. The healing comes from letting there be room for all of this to happen."
—Pema Chodron, *When Things Fall Apart*

Sometimes friendships wane because of arguments; other times, friendships fade simply because life interrupts us. And at the time in our lives, the latter happened between Margherita and me. My life grew chaotic at the same time Margherita went through some personal issues of her own. I spent more than five years without seeing Margherita.

My sessions with Woo-ri remained weekly for a couple of years, and then we switched them to bi-weekly. I thought stretching out time between our sessions made sense. She used our time together to talk about current situations in her life that she struggled with. But I also felt like she was still testing me, to see if she could get comfortable with the idea of sharing all of her secrets with me.

During this time in my life, I went through some huge changes with Miguel. As my boyfriend, Miguel, had been ambivalent about marriage. But several years after we began our "business arrangement" to co-own our home, he presented me with an engagement ring. A few years after that, we married. The change in our marital status didn't remedy the long-distance nature of our relationship due to his worldwide business travel.

Most nights when I returned home after work, I felt not only alone but also lonely. I started filling my time by working longer hours and taking on more clients. But that didn't quelch my emptiness. The loneliness continued under my emotionally-exhausting caseload, and I knew I couldn't sustain my pace given the intense nature of providing therapy. After giving of myself each hour of the day to my clients, I returned home craving someone—anyone—to care for me.

I started to double-down on exploring the healing power of solitude. I read a research paper that equated solitude to a bad-tasting medicine that improves our health over time. This idea sparked something within me. I reframed how I viewed my time alone, and I found a productive, energizing way to fill it. Instead of throwing my emotions into working with more clients to avoid being alone, I embraced solitude as a practice of self-love and healing. Even if no one else gave me a warm hug each day, I could learn to comfort myself.

Do you know how to create a vibrant, textured, stunning flower garden? First, you pick the perfect location, one that will get the required amount of sunlight or shade depending on what you plant. Delicate plants need protection from strong winds, so they don't break or topple over. Next, you prepare the soil, breaking up hard clumps of earth to allow water, fertilizer, and roots to penetrate. Then you're ready to plant choice seeds and bulbs. If you want to grow large purple allium, then plant large purple allium bulbs, not nutsedge or poison ivy. For the next few weeks after planting, you must nurture the new growth with plenty of water and the type of fertilizer your flowers need. Watch the weather forecast, so you don't lose flowers to a late-season hard frost. You also might need to cover them up, so they don't get damaged by the cold. And then? You wait. Some flowers push through the soil quickly, while others take months or even years to develop.

I approached my self-therapy sessions following the same steps I had to build my gardens. While digging in the dirt, I also dug deeply into my childhood, dissecting various painful events from my past. Serving as my own therapist, I found that I made a delightful counseling client. Instead of shying away from topics that hurt my feelings or weakened my self-esteem, I leaned into them so I could better know myself. I lowered my defense mechanisms and answered hard questions. Little by little, some of the damaged parts of me started to mend. I felt less lonely, my garden looked fabulous, and my soul began to breathe again for the first time in years.

When Miguel returned from the road, we made the most of our time—visiting with his family and reconnecting. I started believing that I held the best of both worlds. I had time to get to know myself better, and I had a partner who I could share little joys with.

Difficult, sometimes painful, challenges can follow a period of rapid emotional growth, almost as if the development that occurs inside of us gets forged in the heat of an external, real-world test. Which is what happened next.

Miguel's time at home never seemed long enough, and before I knew it, Miguel had to pack his bags for an extended trip to China.

Even before I met Miguel, he owned a yellow-naped parrot named Buzz. When we integrated our households, we put Buzz's cage in my office where he became my work buddy. Buzz loved to sing, talk (and curse!), and he strutted through the house like he owned the place. Paduki and Buzz became my children. Each morning when Buzz awoke, he'd exit his cage, walk to our bedroom, and climb on top of Paduki who slept by the bed.

Paduki wouldn't move a muscle when Buzz was on top of him. Then Buzz would climb up to the bed to give us kisses while saying, "I love you! I love you!" This was his special way of waking us up in the morning!

Buzz always knew when Miguel planned to leave town, and he grieved. As soon as Miguel's suitcase hit the top of the bed for packing, Buzz started to mourn.

The morning Miguel left for his trip to China, he went to kiss Buzz goodbye. Unfortunately, instead of giving Miguel a gentle peck, Buzz latched onto Miguel's tongue, drawing serious blood.

"Damnit, you fuckin' bird!" Miguel screamed while swatting Buzz away.

I wasn't home when Miguel returned from his trip. Then, without a word to me, Miguel returned Buzz to the pet store where he'd bought him several years earlier.

My heart broke. Miguel had given away one of my children.

Before I could even process the loss of Buzz, Paduki died. Immediately, the house felt like a black hole, void of laughter, warmth, and life. Any love that had existed inside the walls disappeared.

Even with the work I'd been doing on myself, these losses plunged me into deep grief. Years later, I'd read research about how those with childhood trauma often bonded more closely with animals than people. I felt lost when my "children" were no longer in my life.

I didn't wait long until I sought out another golden retriever and brought home Cosmo. Oh, how easy it is to love a puppy! Cosmo brought new life into the home and helped me embrace Eastern teachings, such as the concept of reincarnation. I believed that Paduki's spirit returned in Cosmo's body. The first time I let Cosmo free in the backyard, he ran down the deck stairs, through the gated pool area, and straight to Paduki's grave. Once at the grave, Cosmo kissed Paduki's collar, which was draped over the dog statue that marked the gravesite. Then Cosmo curled up and slept there for the rest of the day.

While Cosmo helped alleviate my grief, my work in the clinic kept pulling down my spirit. By this time, I'd spent the last five years working as a psychotherapist where clients came from a community-based treatment clinic. The clinic further contracted with a group home housing three hundred people with mental illness. Many of the clients came from inpatient psychiatric hospitals from around the NYC area.

One of my first cases was working with a catatonic woman named Kelly. She'd lived at the group home for three years. Her records showed that she never came out of her room. When I visited her in her room, I saw a heavyset woman of about three hundred pounds lying in her bed while cockroaches crawled over her. Careful to avoid the roaches, I sat down on a chair by her bed. She didn't respond to any of my greetings or questions, of course. I didn't know how to work with this woman, yet I was more than motivated to dive into catatonia world.

I began visiting her every day for thirty minutes. Since she didn't acknowledge me, I gave her a running commentary on my day, what I'd seen on the news, my commute, the weather, and things like that. I had no expectations of her, but I wanted Kelly to know that I cared enough to show up and to talk with her. I did this for a month straight.

Then one day, an administrative assistant called my office.

"Hi," she said. After a pause, she said something that I couldn't believe. "Um, Kelly is here to see you."

"Kelly? She came out of her room?" I asked, completely stunned.

I rushed out of my office where I found Kelly standing there.

"Can you help me find my daughter?" Kelly asked.

No one even knew that Kelly had a daughter, much less did anyone expect her to start talking and walking!

After I led Kelly into my office, I learned more about her life.

Prior to moving into the hospital, she'd lived with her daughter and two grandchildren. One weekend, Kelly offered to watch the kids so that her daughter could have a night off to enjoy with her friends. During the night, two armed men broke into the house, tied Kelly to a chair, and raped her granddaughters while she watched helplessly. Later, Kelly covered all the windows in black paint and stopped talking.

Anyway, I tracked down Kelly's daughter. When I got her on the phone, I told her that her mother wanted to see her.

"My mother is back?" Kelly's daughter wept with joy on the phone. "She can communicate again?"

As much as I enjoyed being a part of breakthroughs with some clients like Kelly, I also saw more than my share of heartbreak and stress. We had seven murders onsite during the time I worked there. When the police came to investigate one of those murders, one of my clients confessed to the crime. The woman who confessed had been a nun in her former life, and she had a tiny frame. She wasn't the only person who confessed to the same murder. Another time we found a dismembered body in a freezer, leading to an FBI investigation on the premises. The agents "reassembled" the body in the courtyard, one of the most traumatizing things I'd ever seen.

I can't keep working with such extreme cases, I thought more than once while working there. *I need more tools, more training. I don't feel equipped.*

My search for additional learning led me to a three-year certificate program at the Gestalt Center of Long Island. After my first class there, I realized that the only things preventing me from being a full-time, lifelong student was not having a trust fund. I loved how the center taught concepts and forced us to apply what we'd learned in our own lives.

As part of the study program, each student worked with another therapist to do "inner child" work—exploring the part of us that was still affected by childhood traumas or events. The small group facilitator assigned us to read Alice Miller's book, *The Drama of the Gifted Child*, which gave me understanding about how my childhood experiences set me up for failure in my relationship with Asper. Miller wrote that until people become fully aware of how their early childhood needs may have gone unmet, they often unconsciously look to others to meet those needs.

Good Lord, I thought, *It's true. I'm no different from Woo-ri. I didn't want a husband. I wanted a Daddy Long Legs to come rescue me! And I want to stay grandiose so no one can get close enough to the real me or hurt me.*

Which is what I'd done in my relationship with Asper. I wanted Asper to be my everything—my best friend, lover, mother, father, brother, and colleague. I needed him to fill the holes created in my childhood, a task that no one could accomplish—which doomed our relationship. And I'd projected a similar *save me* mindset onto Miguel.

The book reinforced what I'd already learned about my own grandiosity, while also explaining the context of how I came to adopt this survival strategy. I carried so much internal shame from my youth that my grandiosity served as a wall to keep me from getting hurt as well as a substitute for true self-esteem. Any time my grandiosity failed to protect me, I ran away.

Stripped naked as I internalized this awareness, deep sorrow trapped me in a dark place for three days. I couldn't eat. Guilt and internal rage consumed me. Sitting with Cosmo in an otherwise empty house, the walls caved in around me.

Eventually, I picked myself up and went back to school where I continued to learn about my damaged, emotionally raw inner child. I couldn't change the past, but I could improve my future.

I determined to apply everything I'd been learning in my inner work. As I took a hard look at the ways that I'd failed myself and others in my life, something occurred to me: I didn't know how to be assertive. When my brother beat me, I didn't stand up for myself. Of course, if I'd fought back, he would have destroyed me.

But I didn't even try. When my mother criticized me to her friends when I sang in church, saying, "Heawon cannot sing, and she's so ugly. Why are you clapping for her?" What did I say? Nothing. When my father didn't raise a finger to help me as Young Suk pummeled me, did I challenge him or call him out for his indifference? No. I didn't say a word.

I thought through the numerous times when I should have been assertive but said or did nothing. Then I thought through examples of when I thought I'd been assertive, and I saw that what I'd considered assertiveness came across as aggression or just plain meanness.

You call yourself a therapist? a voice in my head taunted me. *How can you help others when you can't even help yourself?*

I felt like I'd been slapped and had no response to that ridicule. At first.

And then a small voice rose up inside me and replied, *I will fail and suffer, because I am human. But each time, I'll learn from my mistakes and every painful encounter, because I am also strong.*

That wise whisper that came to my defense allowed me to access parts of my life with new insight. I began to own my errors without being grandiose or full of shame. All the things I learned in undergraduate and graduate school came alive for me as if for the first time. I found limitless opportunities to apply what I learned.

For example, Miguel and I rarely argued in the traditional sense. Our most predictable conflict came when I'd ask Miguel to help more around the house.

"I'm not washing the fucking dishes," he said resolutely the next time I brought up helping more with household work. "That's a woman's job."

His language stopped me for a moment. Once I recovered, I pushed back using assertiveness.

"Miguel, your father helps your mother around the house. This isn't 1950. Like you, I have a full-time job, and I come home exhausted. We share the cost of the house, and I feel it's only right that we also share the work to keep the household running."

"You selfish cunt," he spat out before storming out of the house.

In the Korean culture, only the lowest-class, crassest people use such coarse language, the kind that Miguel used regularly to shut me up. And whenever Miguel shouted those words, my Korean upbringing prompted me to see Miguel as low-class and vulgar. So of course, my inner child wanted to run away to find safety.

For years I'd considered leaving him because of these episodes. But my Gestalt therapist helped me uncouple the imprint from my childhood culture from Miguel's outbursts. Yes, Miguel held prehistoric, misogynistic views about housework. And his explosions were both emotionally and verbally abusive. Yet I believed we could make our relationship work. I determined to give our relationship every chance to survive and thrive.

So why did he do it? Because he'd learned that was how to end a conversation he didn't want to have. He didn't have emotional self-regulation or the skills to communicate his wants and needs. So instead of learning new skills, he simply dropped an f-bomb to get rid of me.

I didn't have some magical, psychotherapeutic wand I could wave in Miguel's face to change his actions. But I could use my insight to react differently to him, like I did when I "talked back" to him. Sure, he blew up when I didn't back down, but I was learning how to be assertive without backing down or matching his level of aggression. I was no longer an unarmed victim.

I won't lie. These conflicts took a lot out of me. But I chose to stay with him, at least for the time being, telling myself that I couldn't keep leaving relationships that were imperfect. And a part of me felt the need to do penance for my failed marriage to Asper too. Love wasn't the only thing that had driven either relationship. Scared, insecure, and damaged, my inner child craved a knight to rescue me from my past, even if it meant I got trampled by a few hooves in the process. But if I wished a different future for myself, I needed to navigate the world in front of me instead of trying to change the path behind me.

When Miguel returned from one of his trips, he told me he had an epiphany.

"Heawon, this travel is killing me," he admitted. "It was fine when I was younger, but now it's just a pain in the ass. And I know that when I'm gone for long stretches, you have to do everything around here. It's too much for any one person," he said in a rare show of empathy. "So," he concluded, "I'm going to give it one more year, and then I'm going to quit my job and find something that doesn't require travel."

"That's wonderful," I told him, thrilled that he'd come to this on his own. "I support you whatever you do, but I'd love to have you around more often. I miss you when you're gone."

Miguel then hit the road again, and I attended the summer retreat at the Gestalt Center for all three-year students and faculty. On the first day, we did a physical exercise in the grand hall where we lay down in a circle. The president of the institute attended the session too, and I could see him standing at the other end of the large hall. When the facilitator told us to lay down, the president came all the way from the other end of the hall to lay next me. At the time, it made me a little uncomfortable, but I loved the training and left with invaluable tools.

Summer passed into winter, and the center held another retreat, this one at a three-story house beautifully decorated for Christmas. On the first night, they threw a party that felt like a fancy ball. I stood talking with some of my classmates, then one of the trainers from the center stood nearby to get my attention.

"Hello Heawon," she whispered discreetly in my ear. "The president, Dr. Robert, is looking for you."

"You're sure he wants to see me?" I asked, surprised since I'd only been in his presence one time, earlier in the summer when we'd done the exercise together.

"Yes," she answered, "If you'd just come with me."

She led me to a long wooden table where Dr. Robert sat at the head. Around us, students talked with one another, sipped wine, and enjoyed the décor of the room.

"Would you come here, please?" Dr. Robert said, motioning me to come right next to him.

I took the few steps forward to do as he requested.

He pulled me behind him, placed my hands on his neck, and said, "Would you give me a massage?"

Well, that's just the creepiest thing I've ever heard, shot through my mind. Then another part of me thought, *Don't be so paranoid, Heawon. Just do as he asks.*

Despite my inner conflict, I complied, not knowing exactly how to navigate this moment. But as soon as my hands touched him, I grew mortified and quickly pulled back.

"Excuse me, I must use the restroom," I said as I exited the room.

In the bathroom, I tried to contain my emotions as they flared hot. *Did this female trainer just try to pimp me out? Why did the president just put me in this position of humiliation?*

I immediately flashed back to my childhood—to when my mom told Dad to kiss me instead of her after he returned home drunk. She then blocked father's advance by pushing me at him! So my father kissed me, and not a fatherly peck on the forehead. He thrust his tongue into my mouth so quickly that I couldn't even react at first. Then I pushed him away. He said nothing as he walked away into their bedroom. My own mother and father had subjected me to such cruelty, yet I remained powerless. What could I do? I was eleven years old at the time.

When my mind returned to the present, I knew what I had to do. *I'm no longer a helpless child. I will not be turned into a victim or be forced to tolerate this unwanted advance from Dr. Roberts or his cohorts,* I determined.

I didn't return that night, nor did I complete my certification.

As a child, I'd acquiesce to attempt peace when I found myself in conflict. If that failed, which it usually did, I'd take the abuse—but then obsess about what I'd done to provoke such mistreatment.

But I wasn't a child any longer. I'd found some inner strength. I didn't have to stay in a situation where I felt compromised. And I didn't need to accept any blame either. Instead, I simply walked away.

Most psychotherapists offer compassionate healing to people in their personal struggles. Just a few bad actors can give the whole of psychology a bad name. I refused to let the minority steal the gold nuggets I'd discovered in my studies and on my journey. So even as I left the Gestalt Center, I didn't "throw the baby out with the bath water," so to speak. The president and some of his minions acted like predators, but the concepts I learned and continued to apply in my life and practice empowered me.

I viewed what I learned at the Gestalt Center the same way I looked at my father, "Korean Freud." I didn't respect my father's actions at home, but I appreciated the value of what he'd done for South Korea to advance social work and social welfare programs. And just like I'd had to do with my own father, I could certainly separate the good work from the personalities at the Gestalt Center. I didn't need to be "all for" or "all against." I could savor the morsels of truth I sampled while rejecting a couple of the chefs.

As the daughter of Korean Freud, I'd never considered myself a Freudian therapist. Instead, I enjoyed the works of Freud's student, Fritz Perls, the pioneer of Gestalt theory.

In my inner child work, I saw how I'd dismissed a large part of my Eastern heritage because of a few significant, damaging experiences in my childhood and early adulthood. But in Gestalt therapy, which integrates Eastern and Western philosophy, I became fascinated with the best practices from various disciplines. I learned to incorporate Eastern philosophy, acupuncture, and body work into the more traditional Western healing practices. Gestalt taught me self-awareness about my emotions, perceptions, thoughts, and sensations, and it taught me to be present in the moment.

As the Gestalt Center part of my life ended, I sought out a new learning opportunity. Unfortunately, the stress at work continued to increase. I mentioned the deaths and murders at the group home and clinic. But the final straw for me came when the violence got closer and more personal.

Working at the group home conducting patient discharges on payday, I sat in the leadership meeting in the director's office conducting a patient interview. Payday was a big deal. That's the day the patients lined up to receive allowances from their monthly disability payments.

While we talked with the patient, two men in UPS driver clothing barged in with guns in hand.

"Open the safe," one of the men said, pointing his gun at the director's head. "The rest of you, face the wall!"

Is this it? Is this how I'm going to die? Are they going to shoot us all? I wondered as thoughts raced through my head faster than I could process them. *I have pepper spray in my purse. Should I try to reach my purse? If I'm going to die, should I at least try to fight back?* I thought next.

The gunshot that came as I was thinking about what to do sounded like a cannon firing in that small office. KaBOOM! The wall we faced seemed to bounce from the concussion, and each of us jumped.

"I said, *open the safe. Now!*" the gunman shouted after shooting into the ceiling to prove he'd do whatever was necessary to get the money.

"OK, OK," the director said with his hands up as he moved to the safe. "Take the money and go. No one needs to get hurt," he added.

The director opened the safe, handed one of the gunmen the money, and the two took off immediately. As soon as they left, everyone broke down except me. They were crying, fainting, screaming, or just staring blankly into space

And as the only psychotherapist in the room, I tried to take care of everybody: checking on them, settling them down, holding them, and telling them they were safe and would be okay.

I remembered the story in the Hebrew Bible about Elijah ministering to the widow of Zarephath. The Lord told Elijah to tell the poor widow that neither her flour nor her oil would run dry, allowing the widow to make all the bread she needed to keep her family alive. She kept pouring from the flour and oil, but the jars never ran out.

I was not like that jar of oil. By the time I got home that night, I had run empty. Nothing remained inside of me.

The next morning, I immediately looked for a job outside of the city. I was done with the long commute and the violence. Before long, I was offered and accepted a job at an inpatient rehabilitation facility in a hospital that overlooked Greenport Bay. What a completely different setting! Instead of trains, car fumes, traffic, and crime scenes, I drove on nearly empty streets through picturesque farms to a scenic beach town. When I drove there for the first time, the resort town greeted me with a delightful sight: young children licking ice cream cones and families enjoying the coast.

I quickly learned that summer resort towns such as this had close-knit communities where the relatively few year-round residents knew one another. As the only Asian, I stuck out like someone climbing Mount Everest in a bikini, and I started wondering why I'd even taken the job.

But when the tourist season closed for winter, I understood why the Greenport Bay community needed me. With no winter work, many of the residents spent their days and nights drinking and doing drugs. Even high school students brought water bottles full of vodka to school to drink in class.

Although I brought a dual diagnosis program from the city to this suburb, I wanted to extend my learning to include addiction and recovery.

"You've come to the right place," the HR director told me when I asked about additional training. "We will pay for your education in drug counseling, if you're interested."

"Yes," I said, thrilled at hearing this. "I'm very interested!"

I started attending classes at Pace School for alcohol and drug counseling. Between the new job, my private practice with clients like Woo-ri, and school, time moved both slowly and quickly. Miguel stayed on the road, and I enjoyed my nights studying and cuddling with Cosmo.

A few days after Miguel returned from one of his trips, I remembered that I needed to follow up with him about something.

"Miguel, do you know what today is?" I asked as an opener.

"Oh shit," he said. "It's not our anniversary, is it?"

"No, it's not that," I laughed. "A year ago today, you told me that you would work for one more year, and then you would find a job that doesn't make you travel so much. Do you remember that conversation?"

"Oh, that," he said, rubbing his chin. "I've been thinking that over too."

"What have you decided?" I asked, mindful for the first time in my relationship I neither held nor wanted control over my partner's decision.

"I love my job," he said flatly while plopping on his kitchen chair. "Yeah, I hate the travel, but it's part of who I am, you know? I'm not sure I'd make it sitting at a desk day in and day out. I'd go nuts. So that's what it comes down to. I really love my job, and I want to keep doing it."

"Then," I said, moving behind him, "you should keep working there." I kissed the top of his head, and we never talked about it again.

I was learning.

Chapter Nine

"A sorrow shared is a sorrow halved."
—Proverb

As more time passed, I continued pursuing professional growth and personal healing, making new friends, and seeing my relationship with Miguel change. And I kept meeting with Woo-ri nearly every Thursday at 4:00 pm.

I continued my private practice and took on more clients. Woo-ri continued seeing me, but I grew concerned that our sessions had stopped bringing forward progress. Woo-ri often talked about seemingly unrelated topics, and I wondered if she would ever fully expose her thoughts and feelings to me.

That all changed one Thursday afternoon when she again breezed into my office promptly at 4:00 p.m.

"*Annyeong, chingu.*" I greeted Woo-ri warmly, knowing that *chingu* was a word used when greeting a close friend. After I said that, I questioned why I'd used such a familiar salutation with my client.

My concerns over professionalism and cultural protocols disappeared when Woo-ri returned with her own hearty, "*Annyeong, chingu!*" before giving me a slight bow. Then she caught me off guard by hugging me.

In Korean culture, hugs would take place between married couples and very close friends. While the culture had changed somewhat over time, South Korea was not a nation of huggers.

"Ah," I said, returning her hug. "As always, I'm so glad to see you."

"And I'm glad to have met you," Woo-ri said as she took her familiar place on the sofa.

"I've felt safe sharing with you some of the experiences I've had in my life. And I know the only way I will ever feel whole is if I trust someone enough with my secrets," she said, looking at me with an openness I'd not seen in her before. "Since I've grown to trust you, I think I'm ready to tell you more."

"I would love to hear it," I said, leaning back in my chair and pulling out my notebook.

"If you don't mind," Woo-ri said quickly, "don't write. I want to just talk with you. Like we're friends instead of you a therapist and me, well, a client."

I closed my notebook and placed it on the end table next to me. "It would be my honor to listen as your friend."

"Thank you," Woo-ri responded with a slight nod. "So here goes," she said before she brought me into her childhood with vivid recollection.

Woo-ri's *oppa* (Korean for brother) was born with lovely, fair skin, just like his *umma* (Korean for mother). So of course, Umma adored him. Umma's skin appeared alabaster next to her *appa's* (Korean for father) darker hue.

Years later when Umma became pregnant again, she didn't care if she had a boy or girl, as long as the baby was as beautiful and fair as Oppa. Throughout her pregnancy, she looked up at a picture she'd hung above her bedding of a perfectly white baby.

"Lord, please give me another beautiful baby," Umma prayed. "A beautiful, white baby like my son."

The midwife arrived when Umma went into labor with her second child. The birth of her son had been uneventful, so Umma had no reason to expect that this one would be any different. But she didn't have an easy delivery. After hours of labor, she no longer had the strength to push or even cry out in pain. Then she lost consciousness.

When she opened her eyes, Umma saw nothing except white, sterile walls. A nurse nodded and smiled at her. She'd been admitted into the hospital.

"What happened?" Umma cried out to the nurse. "Why am I here? Where is my baby?"

Panic struck her heart, and she tried to get up before the nurse stopped her.

"Everything is fine now," the nurse assured her. "You have a baby girl. She's very healthy. No problems. But you lost so much blood, the midwife brought you to this hospital to save you. You nearly bled to death. But you and your baby are fine, I assure you."

After hearing that, Umma fell back into her bed and into a long, heavy sleep.

When she finally awoke, her first thought was of her daughter.

"Please bring me my little girl," she pled with the nurse. "I want to see my beautiful baby!"

A few minutes later, the nurse returned with a small bundle in her arms, wrapped snugly in a baby blanket.

"Here's your little angel," the nurse smiled as she gently laid the girl on Umma's chest.

Her eyes grew wide instantly, and then she spoke.

"No, this is not my baby," she said, slightly pushing the sleeping infant away from her body. "You have made a mistake. This cannot be my child," Umma cried out.

After the nurse assured Umma that she'd been very careful to bring her the right child, Umma wailed, "But she's so dark and ugly!" All races and ethnicities, it seemed to her, would prize light skin as beautiful, while dark skin was, well, seen as something lesser. "My baby should be white, like me," Umma insisted. "Like the girl in the picture I have at home."

Umma felt disappointed and angry with her baby. Not only was the infant too dark, but she'd nearly killed her during birth.

As that dark, ugly baby, Woo-ri had inherited her appa's complexion. As the perpetual source of her mother's disapproval, Woo-ri would learn to detach from her emotions to cope with the pain she felt at her rejection.

Once the shock wore off, Umma decided to do her best to love Woo-ri in the hopes that she would grow up to be a beautiful girl with very white skin just like herself. She replaced the photo of the lily-white baby with a picture of swan while dreaming that her own ugly duckling would turn into a stunning white swan.

"Good," she said in a determined voice once she stood back from the photo. "Now we wait for the miracle to happen."

This satisfied Umma enough to go back to her routine. Umma started writing in a diary about the progress her baby made from ugly duckling to swan, but she stopped after a month. Never directly sharing her feelings to anyone about how much she despised her baby girl, Umma pretended that everything was fine. But her judgmental, penetrating eyes and constant insults to her child revealed her true feelings.

Umma's determination failed when her husband came home drunk, which he often did. Part of the South Korean culture at the time was that men worked hard by day and drank deeply into the night. Businessmen might call their gatherings at a bar "the meeting after the meeting." Appa loved socializing, and after a few drinks, he had little interest in returning home.

Her husband returning home drunk was normal, but that night he came home both drunk and aggressive.

"Don't you see?" he yelled at Umma. "We have so much in a land full of so little. What are we to do? What will become of our country if we don't fix it? Are you going to be part of the problem?" he raged on, slurring words that Umma understood but could make no sense of because of his lack of context.

"You!" he stabbed his finger close to Umma's eye. "You are the problem!"

Umma recoiled, having been struck by him during another one of his drunken rages. Later she wrote about the episode in her diary. Then she put the diary aside for many years along with her short-lived determination to love Woo-ri. Instead of writing about her feelings, she turned her negative emotions towards anger directed at Woo-ri.

Umma's scorn of her little girl knew no bounds. She would scrub Woo-ri's skin to make it whiter until the girl would cry in pain. She also would tell Woo-ri to open her eyes when they were already open. Woo-ri's eyes were too small for her liking.

After the Korean War, South Korea struggled economically almost as badly as it had before and during the war. But shortly after turning five, Woo-ri found a treasure inside her own home, one that tempted her like fruit from a forbidden tree had tempted Eve. A guest had brought Woo-ri's family a large bunch of bananas, a quite expensive and exotic fruit that she had never before seen.

"Do not touch them!" Umma issued a stern warning to Woo-ri when she saw her small, craving eyes lock onto the bananas.

Have you ever noticed what people do when they see a "DO NOT TOUCH: WET PAINT" sign on a wall? They touch the wall. And five-year-old Woo-ri, smelling the intoxicating aroma of the bananas, was equally drawn to the forbidden.

After Umma went back about her business, Woo-ri stayed in the kitchen inhaling the fragrance of the fruit. She listened carefully for any sounds that would tell her that Umma was approaching. Hearing nothing, Woo-ri stood underneath the bunch and breathed in deeply.

Heaven, Woo-ri believed. *This must be what heaven smells like.*

Taking one last look over her shoulder, she pulled a banana from the bunch and held it in her hands. It felt soft on all sides except for the end that had attached to the rest of the bunch. That side felt hard and thick.

There are so many of them, Woo-ri told herself. *I want one. Just one. I would share these with my family if they were mine. Yes, I will eat just one.*

Once Woo-ri figured out how to expose the tender, sweet fruit under the tough skin, she took a bite. Oh, how the smooth texture and sweet taste exploded in her mouth! She had previously learned that things that smelled wonderful didn't always taste good, like when she sprayed Umma's perfume in her mouth. But this! Oh, this took her breath away.

After savoring her delicious treat, Woo-ri hid its natural wrapper under trash in the waste bin. Then, Woo-ri went on about her business, which at age five meant either reading or playing alone. Before long though, she heard her mother's feet thundering against the floor, each step getting louder until Umma stood over Woo-ri.

"You!" Umma screamed. "I told you not to touch the bananas! You're such an evil girl!"

Umma must have counted the bananas. Before Woo-ri could apologize or say anything at all, her mother grabbed her by the back of the neck and dragged her to the basement door. Once she opened it, she shoved Woo-ri inside and locked the door.

Woo-ri had always considered the basement as a place of evil. It smelled old, musty, and sour. Since her mother had told her that she'd been an evil girl, Woo-ri imagined that she deserved such punishment. But even knowing that she earned such harsh treatment didn't make her less scared. Noises clicked around her in the dark. *Rats*, she told herself. *Hungry rats that feed on evil girls*, she knew.

Backing up against the wall and wrapping her arms around herself to become as small as possible, she let herself cry and cry. As time passed, she no longer heard scurrying around her. Instead, she heard hushed voices speaking another language, one full of pops and grunts. She pictured monsters sniffing the air to find her so they could eat her. Woo-ri dropped her head to her chest and held her small hands over her mouth so her sobs wouldn't give away her location to the terrible beasts.

Eventually, she cried herself to sleep.

Hours later when her mother opened the door to let Woo-ri out, the girl felt nothing but gratitude to her umma for not letting her die such a terrible death in such a dreadful place.

That night, Woo-ri slept next to her oppa in the living room where she held his hand tightly. She was afraid that the shadows of tree branches on the wall were basement monsters coming back for her. But she convinced herself that if she held her oppa's hand, she'd be safe.

"That's my first childhood memory," Woo-ri said once she finished. "Being locked in a basement for taking a banana. The rest of it I learned from my mom. Of course, my mother told the story differently. In her version, she played the role of heroine for trying to love me, an ugly, ungrateful child. And the things from before I was born and very young, I learned when I read her diary."

I noticed that Woo-ri didn't cry or struggle to speak, as if she'd become so detached from her own story that the events had happened to someone else.

"Woo-ri," I said at last, "I'm so sorry for how your mother mistreated you. "When you shared this story with me just now, what did you feel?"

"Nothing," Woo-ri shrugged. "I'm not five anymore. My

mother broke me down so often that I grew numb to what she did to me. At the time, this made me hate myself. But today, I don't feel any pain from her."

But you carry many scars, I knew.

"Do you still talk to your mother?" I asked.

"Not often," she answered. "I cut off contact with my parents several years ago. But I've talked to them when they had health issues and needed to move into a home. And I spoke to them a few times when they had problems with Oppa."

"It's difficult to cut people out of our lives that we believe we should love and be grateful to," I told her, speaking to myself as much as to her. *I'm learning the same thing*, I acknowledged in my heart. *But Oh Lord, it's hard.*

"I'm glad that you set up a boundary to protect yourself," I added.

"I rarely think about them now," Woo-ri continued. "Well, I guess you would say that I don't *consciously* think about them. But on a *subconscious* level—is that the right word?—I know many of my relationships have been hurt by how my family treated me. I think I don't know how to be in a healthy, normal relationship."

"Thank you for sharing this with me today," I nodded. "How did that feel to be so open about that piece of your childhood?"

"Honestly, I don't know yet," she shrugged. "Right now, I feel great, like I got something off my chest. But I got over my mom's disdain for me years ago. As I've said, I'm sure it still affects me, but I don't think about it. Maybe later today my feelings will change, and I might even regret talking about it with you. But I feel strong for now."

"Again, thank you for sharing," I repeated. "It helps me to know you better and understand the environment that you came from."

Glancing at the clock behind Woo-ri's head, I continued.

"We still have some time left today," I offered. "Would you like to share more? Because I'd love to hear more."

"No, thank you. I told you as much as I planned to share today," she smiled. "Do other clients write down the things they want to talk about with you?"

"Some," I smiled back.

"Do they also practice saying what they want to say before they come, so they can hear what it sounds like?"

"Yes," I smiled widely. "I believe some do that, too."

"Well, if I continue to feel unburdened later after sharing with you today, I will write out other things I want to tell you and practice saying them so I'm ready for next time," Woo-ri laughed.

With that, Woo-ri rose to leave. This time, once again, Woo-ri pushed aside Korean decorum and gave me a 100 percent all-American hug, and she didn't let go for several moments. I hugged her back just as tightly.

After she left, I realized how much I longed for the affection and affirmation that Woo-ri had just given me with her genuine, non-Korean gesture.

Chapter Ten

"That's the thing with fences, though—where properties touch, only one person has to create a divide for both to feel the separation."
—Janice Lynn Mather, *Facing the Sun*

My two teachers at Pace School were amazing. They led the courses, clinical work, and group projects. Even though the focus was on addiction and recovery, they taught me something tangential through their love and warmth. These two women modeled how to build a loving, supportive family. Not only were they experts in addiction and recovery, but they were also equally skilled in inspiring deep bonds between members of our student group and with clients. Even after the program finished, we all continued meeting informally to support one another.

One of the instructors at the Pace School assigned us to read *The Big Book* by Bill W., the book that first introduced the now ubiquitous twelve-steps used for a myriad of addictions. As I read the book, I had an epiphany: *we are all recovering from something*. While I'd never needed to recover from drugs, alcohol, gambling, pornography, or food, I *did* need recovery from childhood trauma and abuse. I realized that the principles spelled out in *The Big Book* could help every human reset their lives while creating more happiness, peace, contentment, gratitude, and community.

As I applied what I learned at the Pace School in my life, someone suggested that perhaps I'd maxed out the benefits from my solitude practices, and it might be time for me to develop broader, deeper friendships. When I thought about it, I realized that I had no friends near me. And my friend groups had been shrinking. Basically, I had Miguel, when he was in town, and Miguel's family. And while solitude gave me time for self-reflection and self-therapy, it limited my ability to foster new rewarding interpersonal relationships.

My friend's right! I need to get a life! I recognized quickly. *I've become a nerdy recluse. When I'm not taking classes, studying, working with clients, and playing with my dog, I just stay at home and analyze myself.*

Then I started thinking about how I would go about expanding my friend group. When I was young, I could make friends with anyone. All I needed was to find an interest I shared with the other person. "You like music? I do too! Let's listen to music together!" And then I'd have a new best friend.

But as I got older, I forgot that friendships are just that simple. *I'm just out of practice,* I assured myself.

Then, of course, since I'd been in the habit of self-analysis, I immediately overanalyzed my past actions to spotlight any underlying personality defects I might have.

Did I stop making friends because of my old defense mechanism, grandiosity? Do I think that I'm so unique and special that the whole world should line up to get to know me?

Then, finally, I stopped spinning inside my head, and I stopped making excuses for *not* making new friends. I began by seeking out people who I had things in common with as well as those I wanted to learn from, such as the medical professionals I met at the doctor's office. Then I became friends with a real estate agent, because, well, you never know when you might be in the market for a new house. Then I started to meet my neighbors. Suburbia, with its attached garages, encourages people to go from their homes to work and back again without needing to set foot on the streets lined with other homes. So I made it a point to say hello to everyone I passed, to become that friendly neighbor with a smile and a kind word like, "I love what you've done with your landscape." Or "I've always admired your home. It's like something I've seen in magazines."

In no time, I got invited to dinner parties at the homes of my new companions and reciprocated by having them over to my house. I started attending a cooking class and even a ballroom dancing class. The dance instructor told me that he was in awe at how well I could follow someone's lead and intention. As I thought about it, having grown up needing to read my brother's mood all the time, I found it easy to anticipate where my dance partner was heading!

As my confidence and skill for social interactions grew, I got a personal trainer to make me a stronger runner. Then I pushed myself outside my comfort zone. For example, I finally learned how to ride a bicycle. Talk about putting fear aside! Then I skied. I snorkeled. And if I'd had an opportunity to skydive and bungie-jump, I'd have done those too. In my now rare times of solitude at home, instead of trying to unravel the mysteries of my mind, I played the piano and sang my heart out as Cosmo howled along in what I can only hope was earnest appreciation.

Miguel was the oldest child in his family, and, as typical in that role, he liked the idea of us hosting his family for each holiday and gathering. Of course, he didn't like the idea of doing any of the work for these occasions. But I didn't mind. These family visits gave me the chance to flex my culinary chops, and I loved cooking for the twenty to thirty family members who showed up. I'd prepare everything lovingly from scratch, selecting three or four entrees for each meal and placing menus at each table setting to create a world-class restaurant experience, as if the food had been prepared by a James Beard Award-winning chef! Then I baked cakes and breads. I never tired of the praise Miguel's family heaped on me doing something that I already loved doing.

Cooking and baking served as my exit strategy from my job stress. Whenever I felt like I was on the cusp of burnout, I imagined myself opening my own restaurant. *A Taste of Heaven. Heawon's Delicacies. The Accidental Chef.* I came up with a long list of potential restaurant names. Just escaping into those thoughts gave me a shot in the arm as if I'd just taken a day off, and my fantasy pulled me through even the hardest days.

Meanwhile, my relationship with Miguel kept changing. And not for the better. His changes in behavior confused me. When we first got together, we spent each night when he was home having dinner together and watching TV. He was deeply affectionate, and his touch could provide me with both pleasure and safety.

Then those things stopped. Instead of coming to bed with me, he'd stay up to spend time alone. I assumed that he needed to catch up on work or wanted to unwind playing a video game.

"Miguel," I said at dinner one night, "I want to talk about our intimacy."

"What about it?" he said while chewing.

"We aren't physical like we used to be," I said, choosing my approach carefully. I intended to make this a productive conversation, not a condemnation session. "We used to go to bed at the same time, and we made love regularly. Now you hardly touch me," I said, certain that my voice conveyed no judgment.

"You want me to fuck you," he snapped. "Is that what you're saying? You want me to perform on command like I'm a stud animal. Is that it, you *whore*?"

"No," I said, cringing on the inside from his coarse language,

"That's not what I'm saying. I want us to reconnect physically like we used to. I need to know that you find me attractive and that you still desire me."

"*Bitch*," he mumbled under his breath. Then he yelled more horrible names at me, tossed his plate of food in the sink, and stormed off until after I'd gone to bed.

After that, I put distance between us. As much as I wanted to be close to him, I wouldn't do it at the expense of my own emotional well-being, which he so easily shredded with his abusive behavior.

Miguel never apologized for that or the many other times he lashed out at me. Instead, he'd wait until I'd seemed to move on. Then he'd make overtures like arranging exotic trips to Singapore, Hawaii, France, Italy, Greece, Malta, Turkey, etc. Did you see how many locales I listed? Yeah, each trip usually happened after he'd ripped my self-esteem asunder.

As a therapist, I recognized the cycle of abuse the two of us were caught up in. But the human part of me didn't care. I wanted to be loved, even if his loving actions surfaced only when he felt guilty. And a tiny piece of me believed that Miguel taking me to travel the world was his way of showing me love. Regardless of his reasons, these trips always sucked me back in.

When I had to, I suffered in silence or pulled away to get through the tough times. And afterwards, I'd allow myself to enjoy the rewards that followed the abuse. But I also started researching communication styles, marriage, porn and sex addiction, anger, and male psychology, all things that helped me personally as well as in my counseling business.

During a time between my abuse and make-up cycle, my CEO at the hospital and addiction rehabilitation center approached me with a request.

"Heawon, I could really use your help. I want to go after this New York State grant," he said as he put a large file in front of me. "It requires an extensive application. You're the most experienced therapist on the team. Would you look it over to see if you think we'd stand a chance of getting it? I don't want to invest too much time if you think it's a long shot."

"Sure," I said, taking the file off his desk. "I'd be happy to. When do you want me to get back to you?"

"Could you have it done by the end of the week?" he asked, flashing a big smile and soft eyes my way.

At first, I gave it a quick glance. Later, I read it more carefully, and I realized I knew nothing about grant writing.

"Well, what do you think?" he asked me when we met again.

"Oh, I don't know anything about grants. If you want me to try though, I will. But I'll need three days off to do it."

"That's great!" he responded enthusiastically.

After I left his office, I walked around the hospital looking like a scared, lost puppy. *Why did I say yes? What was I thinking? What do I do now?* I chided myself.

My friend at the hospital, James, walked past me and noticed my distressed look.

"What's going on, Heawon? You look like you lost something."

"I did!" I explained. "I lost my mind!" Then I told James about how I'd agreed to write the grant for the CEO.

"English is not my first language, obviously," I admitted my deepest insecurity to James. "While I can speak well enough, writing is still very challenging for me. It takes me a long time, and I know I don't always use the best words."

"No problem," he said quickly. "I'd love to ride alongside of you on this project. If you take the lead in writing, I'm happy to look it over when you're done."

I wrote the application and gave it to James to review. He looked it over while I sat next to him at his desk. He asked me a few questions at times and corrected a few words here and there.

"Okay, that line I just read," he said patiently, "can you tell me what that means in more detail?"

He did this several times, mentoring me through the revision in a gentle, almost fatherly way.

When he finished, he placed his warm hand on my shoulder.

"Heawon, I can't tell you how awesome this writing is. It's unbelievable that you came up with a program like this in just a couple of days," he smiled.

I blushed and left his office quickly.

It's hard to put into words what I felt, but it might help to explain the backdrop of this meeting. First, my historical way of masking my insecurities was either to put up walls or become grandiose. This time, I admitted my fears instead of trying to cover them up. That new experience elevated my self-esteem to a higher level. Second, I'd spent the past several years growing my expertise in addiction therapies. As a result, I'd been promoted to the director of the program. Knowing that the CEO of the large organization had followed my career and the success of my department personally gave me another direct boost. Finally, as a therapist, I'd grown accustomed to being the one who did all the giving. I'd bend over backwards to serve my colleagues, clients, and even strangers. This time, I was on the receiving end of kindness from my friend, James.

Now, let me add the most potent element driving my feelings: I found myself uncontrollably attracted to James.

Starting from the moment he sat down with me to review the grant application, I couldn't sleep for three days. My mind became so blurry that I began to hallucinate. No matter what I tried to do, I could not block out thoughts of him. Between my insomnia and obsessive thoughts, I felt like I might experience a psychotic break if I didn't sleep. I couldn't function. My obsession grew to the point where I cut my arms and legs with a knife to try to purge my thoughts of him so I could sleep.

From Gestalt Theory, I'd picked up the life-changing skill of the Contact Cycle. This practice means that whatever crossed into my awareness, I made contact with it. When I felt thirsty, I didn't ignore it and keep working; instead, I stopped and got a drink of water. When I felt tired, I rested. When sad, I cried. The Contact Cycle meant I didn't allow unfinished business in my life. I connected with my emotions directly until they were met naturally.

But what could I do with this obsession?

I thought about what I'd learned by reading the book *Feeling Good: The New Mood Therapy* by psychiatrist David D. Burns, MD. Burns taught me that my emotions were allowed, whatever they were. When I allowed my feelings to flow through me, I opened the door for long, repressed emotions—like the abuse from my childhood—to emerge. The concepts also opened the door to my first panic attack.

I remember highlighting one particularly powerful line in his book: "Your thoughts create your emotions; therefore, your emotions cannot prove that your thoughts are accurate." Since my emotions were spinning around James, I knew that I needed to reframe my thoughts if I were to survive this current crisis.

Piecing together the thoughts that led me to my current, heightened level of emotions, I knew I needed to deconstruct my thinking, challenging the assumptions I'd never fought back against. And then a lightbulb went off as my brain allowed me to rein in my feelings.

Here's what happened, I told myself. *James treated me with the level of tenderness and decency that I always wanted from my parents but never received. I transferred my latent hunger for parental love into obsession when James showed me kindness.*

As I continued to think through my feelings, I reminded myself that Miguel had refused to touch me for years, leaving me lonely and frustrated. *My longing for affection caused me to combine my emotional cravings for parental love with desiring affection from Miguel. Having neither, I've projected this out-of-control desire for a man I hardly knew!*

As my rational brain pulled my emotions back from the edge, I knew what I must do to end my insanity. *I'll talk to James about my internal crisis to explain my behavior and end my obsession*, I told myself. *Then I'll regain my equilibrium.*

"Do you have a few minutes to talk?" I asked James over the phone after I made this breakthrough.

"My day is getting away from me," he said, "but I'd love to meet. Can you do dinner after work?"

I hesitated for a moment and then agreed.

We ordered a bottle of wine, and we both told the waitress our dinner order. While we drank our wine and waited for our food, he started.

"So what is it that you wanted to talk about?" James asked, leaning forward.

After stumbling with my words for a few moments, I started.

"Well, I don't know how this will sound to you," I spoke hesitantly, "but it might help to explain the backdrop to the story." I told him a bit about my relationship with my parents and how I craved their approval and kindness. Then I shared how I felt when he had helped me with the grant application a few days earlier.

"And I think that's how my wires got crossed, you know?" I said with a nervous laugh. "You're such a kind, fatherly man, and you showed such interest in my work that my feelings got ignited. And everything got crossed in my brain. Yes, I find you attractive. But your warmth sparked something inside me beyond anything logical or physical. It just took me a few days to sort out. And I felt like I needed to say something to you, because..."

"Can I interrupt you?" he said, reaching his hand across the table. "I walk through your program a few times a day, right? Why do you think that is?" he asked.

I shook my head, not sure what he was asking me.

"To see *you*," he said, squeezing my hand. "Yes, I've always been a fan of your program. But more than your work, I've been madly attracted to you."

I'm married. James is married. Have we just admitted our

mutual attraction to one another? This is not right. Now what? I wondered, having no experience with this kind of situation.

We ate dinner and kept the conversation mostly about work. Afterwards, he walked me to my car.

When I got home that night, I felt exhilarated…and ashamed. But mostly exhilarated. Yes, I knew it was wrong. And yes, I felt terribly torn up about it.

I'd practiced journaling for years as part of my self-therapy, and I wrote the details of the evening into my computer. I spared nothing. As soon as I saved the entry in my journal, I switched off the computer and got the soundest sleep I'd had in weeks.

Of course, I wouldn't have slept at all had I known the storm that was approaching.

Driving to work the next morning, my phone rang. Looking down, I saw it was Miguel calling. He'd been home from travel for the last few weeks.

"Hello, Miguel," I said cheerfully.

"I read what you wrote last night," he said slowly in a low voice. "About your little 'date.'"

"I'm coming home as soon as I can," I said quickly. "We'll talk when I get there, OK?"

My mind raced along with my heart. In trying to get my own needs met, I'd hurt Miguel deeply. I'd been selfish. I wanted to disappear.

But it was a payday, and as the director, I had to complete staff timecards. I rushed inside, finished my work, told the staff I had an emergency, and rushed home.

"What happened?" Miguel asked in a stony voice when I walked in the door.

"Well, you read what happened," I said, having no defense for my actions.

Without saying a word, he left the room and returned with a large box of papers.

"What's that?" I asked.

"All of your email correspondence with your friends and journal entries over the last six years," he said.

He'd monitored every communication, each keystroke I'd made for the last six years. That's when I discovered that my marriage had more problems than I knew.

Chapter Eleven

"What lies behind us and what lies before us are tiny matters compared to what lies within us."
—Ralph Waldo Emerson

Yes, Miguel had physically abandoned me for some time, but that was not an excuse. I accepted full blame for my physical and emotional betrayal. The two of us committed to work through our problems and stay together. But we both knew that things needed to change. I quit my job at the clinic that I loved to remove myself from James, who I'd crossed the line with, and Miguel and I became a little more open with one another.

Miguel lost his job when the tech bubble burst. He found another job making far less money, but I didn't care. At the same time, since he no longer travelled, we were together all the time, which magnified our existing marital problems. As much as I wanted to assert myself and tell him directly what I needed from him, he continued to call me names and scream when his mood darkened.

And I took it. I carried so much shame for my behavior with James that I felt I deserved his mistreatment.

But things escalated quickly. During an argument, Miguel put his hands around my neck. I grabbed his wrists and pushed him back. I might as well have been a gnat trying to swat an elephant. But after he felt my hands on his wrists, he snapped back to his senses and let go.

You brought this on yourself, I condemned myself. *Be patient and forgiving with him. You're the one who crossed the line. He has every right to be angry with you!*

Several months later, Miguel and I were eating dinner at a Japanese restaurant. I told him that I got a call from my mom earlier in the day. I felt like I had to take her call when she rang, since it had been more than ten years since I'd spoken to her. On that call, Mom told me that Dad was in declining health, that they were moving into assisted living, and that they found themselves in financial straits. Even though I'd promised myself not to get sucked into my family's drama after all the work I'd done to distance myself from some of the darker moments of my past, my heart as a daughter and therapist kicked in, and I wanted to help.

"My parents are struggling," I said, giving him a short summary. "I think I might need to go back to South Korea to help them."

"What? Are you *stupid*?" he asked angrily, just loud enough that I wondered if others in the restaurant heard. "Why would you want to help them?"

I tried to explain myself to Miguel, but regardless of what I said, he argued with me. He didn't have the ability to verbally express his feelings, so he didn't use cogent words or show me empathy. Rather, he just raged quietly—eating but saying nothing. I ate my meal as quickly as possible so we could get out of this uncomfortable situation.

When we got home, Miguel entered the house first and I followed him, closing the door behind me. But the wind blew strongly that night, and it slammed the door shut hard, knocking a painting off the wall. Miguel assumed I'd slammed the door out of anger. He turned around quickly, placed his hands around my throat, and choked me.

I broke free of his grip and yelled, "That's it!" He had pushed me over my limit. I could understand his anger at my emotional infidelity, but I would not tolerate physical abuse.

"I made a promise to myself that I would never allow myself to be abused again. If you're willing to go to therapy with me, I'm willing to try to work this out. But if you refuse, I'm leaving."

He stood his ground for a moment, waiting for me to crack under his glare. Then his face began to soften.

"OK," he nodded. "Yeah, I know I shouldn't have put my hands on you. Make us an appointment, and I'll go."

I thought the first couple of sessions went well. At the second session, the therapist, to use Miguel's language, "called him on his bullshit" excuses about why he got violent with me. At the third session, Miguel didn't show. I felt sick in my stomach. When I got home, I saw a receipt from a local restaurant on his dresser. Apparently, he went to a restaurant and enjoyed a nice meal with a drink while I sat alone in the therapy session. I felt betrayed.

That was that.

I loved Miguel, but in the sixteen years we'd been together, I'd learned to love myself even more. I knew that the time had come for me to divorce Miguel. His parents had been my rock for years. I saw them even more regularly when Miguel was out of town, and I'd told them when we'd gone through problems.

"I don't know if I can stay with him," I confided in Miguel's mom.

"He can be a bully," his mother nodded. "But no matter what happens, honey, you're always family. You will be part of our family forever."

Of course, that all changed when Miguel and I split up.

"Is this about money?" Miguel's mother asked me when I called her to tell her that we were getting divorced.

"What!?" I exploded in shock. "I've been talking to you for

years about our problems. Your son *choked me twice*. He's refused to go to therapy. And you think it's about money? I've been making more money than Miguel for years, and that has never bothered me."

Miguel's parents had sided with their son and listened to whatever reason he gave them about why I'd been such a terrible wife. Facts and families often operate in different orbital planes. Truth is not stronger than blood.

The last time I saw Miguel, he turned and looked at me for a couple of moments. Then he shrugged and said, "I know how important family was to you, so I gave you my family. I thought that was enough."

That was probably the first time in my life I wholly felt the role of the *poor immigrant*. The *white man* had decided what was *good enough* for me, rather than taking me as his equal to decide for myself. He'd thrown me his family like a cruel man might toss his dog a bone, all while continuing to neglect and abuse me.

My next thought reduced my criticism of Miguel and caused me to focus on my decision to be with him. I'd been attracted to him to fill the role of my very own Daddy Long Legs, rescuing me by buying out Asper's share of the house. His financial contribution allowed me to stay in the house I loved, and he filled a void in my life, giving me companionship when he was around. But as time passed, I became more self-reliant.

Asper wanted to be my hero. Miguel wanted to possess me. I'd wanted and found two Daddy Long Legs. But what I really needed was a partner to come alongside me as an equal.

Once I knew that the path to saving myself meant that I must leave Miguel, I accepted that I had to let go of Miguel's family too. Despite their recent harsh words, I loved them like my own blood, and the loss was staggering. I ached all over, knowing how all of them would be together enjoying holidays, while I—the former host of most events—would be an outcast. But as much as I loved

Miguel's family, I knew that my relationship with them couldn't make up for the loneliness I'd experienced with Miguel.

Miguel didn't object to me keeping one family member as my own: Cosmo.

Thirty years earlier when I'd first come to the US to attend Adelphi University in Garden City—landing at JKF with two suitcases in a new, foreign country where I didn't know a soul—I saw these sprawling ranch houses and dreamt that I'd live in one someday. These old ranch houses held a charm I didn't feel for the big mansions and old gothic homes.

After Miguel bought me out of the house, I bought one just like the ones I'd always dreamt about. I finally had a chance to live that part of my dream.

In fourth grade, I'd first imagined myself working in private practice providing therapy to those who were hurting, conflicted, or needing direction. After leaving my job at the hospital, the CEO told me that he would be fine with me asking any of the patients I saw in outpatient services to follow me to my private practice. Even though I now lived a two-hour drive away from the clinic, all of my clients came with me. They didn't mind the drive. They followed me because we'd built a solid relationship, and they wanted to continue making progress. Remembering how I was fired three times from internships at Adelphi because I struggled to speak English and how devastated I was thinking I wouldn't be able to live my dream, I remembered the legendary turtle. It took time, one step a day, and I finally won the race!

I worked in a field I loved, one where I could learn how to better care for myself and my clients. I found an office space with another clinician, and we shared expenses while seeing our own clients. I now lived and worked my dream full-time.

All through my early years, I'd pictured having a large, loving family. I'd married into large, loving families twice. And even though they were fleeting, I got to enjoy the love of family for many years. Of course, I'd pictured having my own children too. Given the history of abuse in my family, I decided I needed to let go of that dream. I was sure that my anxiety and fear would be passed on directly to my kids, if I had any.

But sitting in my new home that first night with my arms wrapped around Cosmo, I realized that I'd experienced variations of every dream I'd ever have.

"Who's my baby boy?" I asked Cosmo as he kissed my face. "You are, Cosmo. You're Mommy's little sweetie."

I'd continued to look within myself for strength, hope, faith, and love with the help of forever faithful and loving Paduki and now Cosmo. My furry children repeatedly taught me about the unending love and loyalty. We shared total trust in each other for protection and love.

I used this time to get to know myself better.

As hard as it was for me to be "partner-free" for the first time in several years, I found it liberating to stop accepting the unacceptable. Once again, I leaned into the solitude. I challenged those voices criticizing me from all angles that said things like, "You're *how* old? And you still have no one?" and "You're unlovable. No one loves you, and no one ever will."

I spent many hours of my self-therapy taking walks and runs. During these "sessions," I observed the regal resilience of nature. I saw various trees with broken limbs, cut branches, and scars on their trunks. I passed little trees, big trees, skinny trees, fat trees, flat shrubs, tall shrubs, those with round leaves, angular leaves, and no leaves. None of them complained about being "less than." Instead, they stood or leaned any way they could, stretching out their arms into the sky towards the sun.

I am one of those trees with broken limbs that doesn't grow as straight as some of the others. But I am enough. In my own way, I am regal in my existence. My parents may never have told me this, but I am sufficient, I told myself each time I spotted a tree that looked unlike those around it. And each time, I would stretch my arms to the sky, look towards the sun, and say, "I am enough."

As a child, my mother had deemed me a deviant when I expected to be respected the same way men were respected. My dad brought home our first television when I was six years old, and Young Suk and I couldn't get enough of it! It was like a magic box that opened the world to us.

One afternoon, my mom asked me to help her prepare dinner for some guests of my father's. My brother and I were watching *World Cup Soccer*, which was huge in Korea.

"Will Young Suk be helping too?" I asked.

"No!" my mother snapped back at me. "Kitchen work is not for a boy to do."

"Then I won't help in the kitchen either," I said defiantly.

My mom beat me for disobeying her. Other relatives criticized me for not "acting like a girl." It seemed to me that "acting like a girl" meant doing all the work so the males didn't have to lift a finger. I didn't agree with that way of thinking, and I chose not to adhere to such nonsense.

Each time I lifted my hands towards the sky, I felt the same elevation I did when I'd first defied my mom by choosing not to be treated as "less than."

In addition to self-therapy, I indulged in self-care by spending time with those in my inner circle. My social life stayed busy, and I continued to make new friends regularly. Since my new home was close to the harbor, I met many new people on my runs there.

On one of my runs around the harbor, I met a man named Alan who rode his bike along the same route. That day, the planets aligned, and we ended up speaking.

"Well, I started out in social work at Adelphi University," Alan answered when I asked him his background.

"Really?" I said, thrilled at how the universe put us on a collision course that morning.

"Yeah, I went to the School of Social Work there. But I changed directions before I graduated and decided to pursue teaching," he told me.

"I attended Adelphi, too!" I responded. "But I stayed in social work and never left."

I learned that Alan and his wife, Sophi, had both retired. They soon became my newest friends.

I also met Greg, a well-known local who wanted nothing more than to create a park in our area. He modeled his plan after Central Park in Manhattan, albeit on a much smaller scale, and spent years turning his vision into a reality. Thanks to his efforts, my town built a park that became a meeting place for many of us locals to enjoy nature. Greg's home overlooked the harbor, and he often hosted informal gatherings at his house where he poured wine for any of us who showed up to share his view.

Later I met a man named Tony whose house overlooked the beautiful Mt. Sinai Harbor. I learned that he chopped and sold firewood year-round. Tony became my firewood supplier.

Of course, I had the most wonderful friends across the street from my house. Linda and Chris were there when I moved in. We were of similar ages and had the same love for furry animals, flowers, and birds. They became my surrogate family, sharing tears as well as laughs. Years later, they would be there when Cosmo died, and they remained available to care for my three cats when I went out into the world to explore, and they were there for anything I went through. Linda and Chris have been much more reliable than my own family had ever been!

I quickly learned that solitude didn't mean loneliness. I lived alone with Cosmo, but I was never lonely. I lived in a small, active community of loving, caring people who made my life feel rich. My new home gave me the perfect blend of solitude and friendship.

I finally realized that I had become my own Daddy Long Legs.

I was whole, just as I was. I was imperfect, to be sure, but I didn't need to or want to be rescued. I completed myself.

The final point of contention between me and Miguel had involved my parents, and more specifically, my desire to help them if I could. After leaving Miguel, I decided to visit my parents in South Korea. I learned that they had to sell their house and move into an assisted living facility outside of Seoul.

As I prepared for the trip, I kept remembering the times in my childhood when they weren't there for me. I could never forget the physical abuse I suffered at the hands of my brother and their unwillingness to intervene. While I returned to South Korea to help them, I took the opportunity to confront them about the abuse I experienced in my childhood. I didn't go into details, but I felt it important to lay out the ways they had traumatized me as a child.

"I'm sorry for how hurt you felt, Heawon," my mother told me, lowering her head.

"I'm sorry, too," my father added. "I have no excuse for how I allowed your brother to treat you like that. I'm sorry for how hurt you felt."

"I accept your apologies," I nodded back. "I wanted you to acknowledge the past, but only so we can begin a new chapter together."

Their acknowledgments of how they'd fallen short during my childhood didn't erase my pain. Feeling sorry for "how hurt I felt" wasn't the same as saying, "I'm sorry that we failed to protect you and love you as we should have." But their pseudo-apology was enough for me to give them a chance to rebuild our relationship.

They caught me up on their lives and told me about Young Suk. I knew that Young Suk had married and had a daughter, Haena. But I learned that years earlier, Young Suk's wife had showed up at my parents' door barefoot in the middle of the night, holding her infant. After returning home drunk, Young Suk had picked up Haena and thrown her against the wall. Then she scooped up her child and ran to my parents' house to keep Young Suk from killing the child. My parents weren't willing to help her, so she ran away with her baby and divorced Young Suk.

"Where is Haena now?" I asked, breathless as I relived my own terror from Young Suk's abuse.

"We don't know where they are," my mom told me. "Your brother's drinking got worse, and he borrowed money from very bad people. Korean mafia. He embezzled and had to make payments to people if he didn't want to go to jail multiple times," she added.

Then they told me that Young Suk had told the mafia where my parents lived.

"We had to pay those men for Young Suk's debt, or they said they would kill your brother," my father said. "We sold our house to pay the debt, but it still wasn't enough. Then they started threatening us. That's when we decided to move into assisted living, so we might have some protection."

After they moved, they cut off all contact with Young Suk too. Once I learned that, I felt safe enough to maintain contact with my parents. One of the reasons I'd broken off regular communication with them was that I didn't want Young Suk to find me.

When I returned home, I started calling my parents weekly to check on them. This gave me an opportunity to practice setting my boundary with them while also keeping our relationship alive.

During this time, my creativity underwent a renaissance, and I took time to decorate my home, cook new dishes, dress with a more artistic flare, and explore hobbies and spirituality. I started the daily practice of emptying my mind from constant thoughts and learned to enjoy physical labor. This period of blooming gave me a new sense of peace and happiness. I became a minimalist as I rid my home of "stuff," so I could enjoy more empty space. Although I continued to work six days a week, I felt renewed when

I got home after a long week, and I looked forward to my time cleaning the house, pulling weeds, planting flowers, collecting leaves, cutting trees, and cooking exotic foods.

As my birthday approached, I planned out my whole day. I would spend the morning at the harbor reading a book under the bluest sky in the full sun. Then I'd return home to make fresh salsa. Then I'd sit in the sunroom with salsa, chips, and a fresh margarita. Cosmo would sit with me, watching the birds and the deer. I no longer looked forward to grandiose or vast events; instead, I learned to savor everyday joys. And the best part of what I planned to do on my birthday is that I could do it more than once each year. My plans were obtainable and replicable, and they required nothing besides me, Cosmo, and the sun.

Probably because of my renewed connection with my parents, I started thinking about Young Suk again. And my nightmares returned, ones where he found me and wanted to kill me.

Instead of allowing fear to trap me, I purchased a rifle and took classes on how to use it. Of course, I never wanted to use it, but the process of purchasing it and learning to use it empowered me and told me that I could take care of myself.

Besides the return of my nightmares about Young Suk, talking to my parents about Haena had created something deeply moving inside of me. Lying in bed thinking about Haena, I had a clear realization of my purpose on this Earth.

For years, I'd wondered, *God, why did you let me live through so much trauma but kept me from having a family of my own?* In a flash, that thought got replaced with something positive. *God, you put me here to be alone. Whenever I asserted my own will over my life, I made unwise choices and suffered even more. But now I see that you made me to be alone, so I could be the family to those who are lonely and broken. You've created me so I can weave in and out of people's lives when they most need love.*

From that moment on, I felt even more honored for having the opportunity to serve others. Whenever I saw a bee or butterfly flitting from flower to flower, I'd say to myself, *I am a pollinator. Whatever I collect from one flower, I give to another that needs what I possess.*

In addition to having utter clarity of my life's purpose, I now had a new mission. "I don't know where you are, Haena, but I will find you."

Chapter Twelve

"An unhappy childhood compels you to use your imagination to create a world in which you can be happy. Use your old grief. That's the gift you're given."
—Sue Grafton

When I learned that Woo-ri had scheduled a session with me for the upcoming Thursday at 4:00 p.m., my heart grew happy. Our weekly meetings had gone to biweekly before they changed to monthly. During a session where she talked about her parents, she cried bitter tears. And then she missed our next two appointments. I started wondering if she'd been avoiding me.

"Oh, no!" Woo-ri responded when I asked her if our last session had scared her off. "No, we had a good session! I hope you didn't worry. I've been very busy. That's all."

"I'm so glad to hear that," I smiled as she took her familiar seat. "How have you been besides busy?"

"Good, good," she answered with a broad smile. "I've been working long hours and spending the rest of my time in nature. I find hiking in the woods so freeing, almost healing."

"I completely agree. I think we share a love of nature from our

South Korean roots, where we could go from the middle of the city to the mountains within minutes," I told her as I remembered how the hills were an escape for me too as a child.

"So," Woo-ri said, indicating that she wanted to change the subject, "I've been thinking more about my childhood since we last met. Maybe because my birthday is coming up. That's always a sad time for me."

"Why does it make you sad?" I asked, wondering if Woo-ri thought about how each passing year brings us closer to our eventual deaths.

"It reminds me of being a child in South Korea," she answered. "I hated my birthday."

"Would you like to say more about that?" I asked to prompt her.

"OK," Woo-ri shrugged. "I don't know how much I will be able to get through today, but I wanted to share a couple of things that I've been remembering from my childhood."

"I understand," I inserted. "This is a safe place. You may say anything you wish. I won't judge you."

"Well, my oppa and I had been close when we were little. He was only a few years older than me, and we were inseparable. Since Appa and Umma moved us frequently, Oppa and I had only each other to play with."

"When it came time for Oppa to go to school, my parents sent him to a private academy so he would get the best education," Woo-ri said.

"That must have been very expensive," I responded.

"It was," she nodded, "and my family never had much money. Of course, our country was still recovering from the Korean War, and we were all quite poor. I never knew wealthy people as a child. We had no television, radio, or even toys. But my parents always found a way to give Oppa the best of everything. They even sent him to a top dojo so he could learn tae kwon do and make more friends."

"Did that make you feel resentful of your oppa?" I asked.

"No. I never even thought about how my parents treated me and Oppa differently when I was a child. I just thought that all parents loved their firstborn sons more than any other child in the family. I didn't know anything different from that. I guess the reason I think about that today is that I was lonely after Oppa went to school. And even lonelier when he started taking tae kwon do lessons in the evenings. He showed me what he learned in class when he came home. I had no one to play with. The only friends I had left were the bugs, and my only toys were the art canvas of dirt on the ground I could write on with sticks."

Woo-ri went on. "When I finally got to attend kindergarten, I went to a public school instead of the fancy school like my brother. I loved everything about school. There I made friends and got out of the house. My kindergarten had a large, lovely playground, and even on Sundays, I would go there to play."

"So you lived close to your school?" I asked just to show her that I was tracking with her story.

"Oh, yes," Woo-ri nodded. "It was maybe a ten-minute walk in a residential area. Since it was Sunday, there was no traffic or noise. I felt completely alone."

Then Woo-ri's face turned dark. "But one time, I wasn't alone. After I played for maybe a couple of hours, I started walking home. Do you remember being five?" Woo-ri asked, not expecting me to answer. "You know, I was so lost in my head, stopping to look at every tree, dreaming about what I wished I could eat for lunch, and skipping along as my mind drifted away." She seemed a bit lost in her memory at this point, her eyes looking upward as if she were staring through the wall.

"'Hello,' an old man smiled and nodded at me as I walked past him," Woo-ri said, shifting in her seat. "'Hi,' I returned without a care in the world. But that changed when he reached out and grabbed me around the waist. I let out a little scream, but he lifted me off the ground and started running with me on his shoulders.

He almost made it to the woods away from the houses. With each step he took, he knocked the air from my lungs, and I couldn't breathe," Woo-ri said as tears filled her eyes.

"Oh my goodness, you poor child," I said to remind her that she was in a safe place now, far away from the woods and that man.

"And then I remembered what Oppa did in his tae kwon do class. 'Kiai!' I screamed as I hit the old man's wrist as hard as I could with the flat of my hand," Woo-ri said, looking at her hand and making a small fist. "And then he dropped me. He didn't let go, but he dropped me enough that my feet reached the ground. As soon as my foot hit the ground, I started running away. Then I ran and ran as fast as I could, and I didn't stop until I got inside my house. When I got home, I ran to where my parents were sitting, and I told them everything. 'A man. He grabbed me. I hit him! Got away! So scared,' I said as I tried to catch my breath."

"And do you know what Umma did?" Woo-ri asked. "She shook her head and walked away in disbelief."

"But Appa asked, 'You hit him?' And I said, 'Yes, I screamed, *Kiai!* And I hit him as hard as I could.'"

"'Hahahahahaha!' my dad laughed. 'That is most excellent! You used tae kwon do!'"

"Did your dad go looking for the man who grabbed you?" I asked, eager to know what happened next.

"No," Woo-ri shook her head. "Neither of my parents showed any concern or gave me a hug. Appa laughed, which was I guess his way of saying he was proud of me, but I wanted him to hug me and say, 'I am so glad you are safe!' Then I wanted him to chase after that old man. But he didn't. I was so scared, but my parents didn't seem bothered by it. I felt almost invisible."

"I'm so sorry that that happened to you," I said sincerely. "And I'm sorry your parents didn't make you feel safe."

"I learned that I needed to take care of myself," Woo-ri continued. "So I stopped going to the playground on weekends. I would only be on the playground on school days when all the children were playing there. And I stopped expecting my parents to protect me. I knew that I would have to take care of myself."

"What a large responsibility for a little girl to take on," I said, shaking my head at Woo-ri's strength.

"But the funny thing is, I never stopped hoping that my parents would care for me like I saw other parents caring for their children. I once heard a song that I think describes me: 'Cockeyed Optimist.'"

"When Umma locked you in the basement, you never told Appa, did you?" I asked directly.

"No," Woo-ri shook her head. "Why? What good would it have done?" she asked rhetorically.

I can see why you wouldn't, I thought. *Growing up in a family where others seemed to care about themselves and not each other.*

"So that was kindergarten, OK? The next year, I started elementary school," Woo-ri continued with her story. "I couldn't sleep the night before. I was too excited with thoughts. *Will I meet new friends? Will they like me? Will we play together? Will I make a special friend that will be my friend forever?*" Woo-ri reflected.

"I knew that each school year had a picnic where students and teachers would eat together and then explore a nearby mountain for the day! So how could I sleep?" Woo-ri asked with a smile. "Did they do that when you were in school?"

"Yes," I smiled. "I remember how it was a big day for not only the students and teachers but for their families."

"Some families," Woo-ri said, holding up her hand. "The day started off great. I was so happy when Umma got up early to make me a special lunch for my first day: *kimbap*," Woo-ri said, reliving her memory of a Korean dish of cooked rice, vegetables, and meats rolled into dried seaweed and then sliced like sushi.

"When I arrived at school, I ran to join my classmates, but as I approached, I saw bigger people huddled close by, all smiling and hugging their children," Woo-ri face grew confused. "Then I understood. The picnic day of school was a big deal. Each child stood with their families, some of them with three generations—parents, grandparents, and great-grandparents—in a group. And there I stood all alone. My mom didn't come. After she made me *kimbap*, she went back to bed, saying she didn't feel well. I didn't even know that families were invited to the picnic."

"And you were all alone," I said sympathetically.

"Yes, and I was embarrassed. Even as a child, I thought how my being alone meant that no one loved me. And that everyone in the school knew that I was unloved and maybe unlovable," Woo-ri said. "So I acted as if I didn't care. Instead of standing close to the families, I went off by myself and pretended that I was too good for any of them."

Maybe the start of acting grandiose to deal with rejection, I wondered to myself.

"But I did care," Woo-ri said as a tear ran down her cheek. "I wanted to hide so no one could see me. I felt unlovable, and I knew that there must be something wrong with me, or else Umma or Appa would have come with me."

Woo-ri cried for a few moments and reached for a tissue.

"You must have felt so alone!" I offered as comfort.

After wiping her eyes, Woo-ri shifted in her seat.

"I told myself, 'Next year will be different. Umma will feel better, and she will join me on the picnic day.' But the next year, she felt too sick to even make me lunch, much less come to the picnic with me. So, while everyone sat laughing and eating with their families, I sat by myself on the mountain with no family or food. I kept my eyes on the ground, not wanting to catch the eyes of any of my classmates and see a look of pity on their faces."

"That's a very sad memory," I said softly. "I'm so sorry that no one made you feel loved on that special day."

"But the mountain did," Woo-ri said, trying to smile. "The mountain became my friend. For a time, at least. Once I stopped going to the playground, I would go to the mountain to play. Oppa and I made some friends in our neighborhood. The mountain held the best hiding places where we played hide-and-go-seek after school. The mountains were better than any playground," she said while staring off.

"I'm glad you have those good memories," I said encouragingly. "What else can you tell me about your childhood?"

"Well, I told you about my birthday coming up," Woo-ri said, pulling her legs up to her chest and wrapping her arms around her knees. "I know that most children love their birthdays. But I never did. One year, I received a gift: a paper doll. That was the only toy my parents gave me during my entire childhood," Woo-ri spoke with a sad voice. "Nowadays, kids have so many toys that they can't walk through the house without tripping over them. But I never had to worry about tripping over my toys, because I never had any until I got that paper doll. You can't imagine how much I loved it," Woo-ri said as she pictured her young self with her doll.

"Since that was my only toy, it became the new center of my world. I got very creative. I found some paper, and I made costumes and outfits for my paper doll, so she had several changes of clothes. I named her Sarang (which means "love" in Korean), and she became my best friend.

"Then we had family visit us," Woo-ri's tone shifted. "Thinking back, they must have had more money than my family, because my cousins wore nicer clothes. Anyway, I was playing with Sarang when my cousin came into my room and grabbed my doll. Then she ripped Sarang up and threw her on the floor," Woo-ri said as new tears formed in her eyes.

"Even now it makes me cry, just thinking about it," Woo-ri said as she wiped her face. "My heart broke into a thousand pieces. My parents treated me like I was crazy for being so sad. They didn't understand the depth of my hurt over the doll," Woo-ri said. "They didn't understand that the little paper doll was symbolic of their love for me: ephemeral and fragile," she added softly.

"That is so sad, Woo-ri," I said as tears entered my own eyes.

"So I hate my birthday. The one present I received as a child got destroyed in front of me," Woo-ri said soulfully. "No, my parents didn't make me feel special, even on my birthday."

I nodded silently.

"But Umma, she was really something else," Woo-ri continued. "She did have one ritual that she performed every year on my birthday. She'd take to lying down in her bedroom, sometimes even a couple of months before my birthday. But on my birthday, she'd call for me to come to her. Then when I sat next to her, she'd say, 'Woo-ri, do you know that you nearly killed me when you were born? I just wanted a beautiful, white baby, one that would make me happy. But then you came out, all dark and ugly, and you took half of my insides with you. I bled so much the doctor thought I would die. You be thankful I had you, Woo-ri! No other mother would have endured so much pain for their child.'"

"How did you respond to her saying that to you?" I asked.

"I never knew what to say, so I said nothing. I just looked at the floor. I tried to avoid her on my birthday, because I knew it was coming. But she always remembered to call me in just to remind me that I almost killed her on the day I was born. It was like her... what's that Catholic training? Oh, catechism! She would repeat that like a catechism on every birthday until I left home. What could I say to something like that?" Woo-ri asked, seeking some understanding of her mom and her loveless childhood. "Was I supposed to be grateful that she gave birth to me? Should I have apologized for nearly killing her?"

"I don't know what you could have said that would have made either you or your mother feel better," I shrugged. "It sounds like your mother felt traumatized by nearly dying. But I don't know what she wanted from you, a child, or what she expected you to say to her."

"I never responded," Woo-ri shook her head. "I just stared at the floor." Then Woo-ri straightened up in her seat as a wry smile crossed her face. "So today, the only joy my birthday brings each year is knowing that if my mother wanted to talk to me, I wouldn't have to take her call."

"It's so hard to set boundaries," I said, pulling from my own recent discoveries. "But it's worth it. You're worth it. You can love other people, but you must find ways to love yourself first. I get the sense that your mother would never be happy, because happiness is an inside job, you know? She would be only as happy as she decided that she would be."

"I know that now," Woo-ri nodded slowly. "I love many things about my South Korean heritage, and I wish I could say that my family was one of the things I loved most. But I've told myself that they've given up the right to have a relationship with me. Do you think that's wrong of me? Is that too extreme to cut off my parents?"

"That's a very deep question," I said, trying to stall while I thought of what to say next. "I think it's different for everyone. If staying in contact with your family drains you emotionally and makes you relive past trauma, I think you're wise for limiting contact with them. If you choose to be in touch with them, do it on your own terms, not because you expect something from them, or they expect something from you."

"I get very emotional when I talk about my childhood," Woo-ri said. "And I get even more emotional when I'm home alone *thinking* about my childhood. I normally have a good memory. Why is it that almost all my childhood memories are sad? Is that normal?"

"Well," I sat back in my seat, "I can answer that in a couple of ways. One, psychologists say that our brains hold something called a negativity bias, where it's easier for us to remember the bad or sad things that happened to us than the positive, happy events in our lives. That's just a function of our brains. We don't control that. It just happens," I said. "Two, I think traumatic events are made memorable in our brains so we can try to avoid recurring trauma. You said you tried to avoid your mother on your birthday, because you knew she was going to traumatize you. You remembered that and tried to avoid it from happening again. Sometimes, like where you are in your life today, those memories can keep you from getting hurt again."

"I didn't have a happy childhood," Woo-ri explained plainly. "Will I ever stop wishing that I did?"

"I don't know that the emotional pain you felt as a child ever completely goes away," I said honestly. "But I like to think of painful memories as something that instructs us. It teaches us how to stay safe in the future. Just like you learned to not count on your parents. It doesn't make the ache go away, but it forced you to learn how to take care of yourself."

"I must be a slow learner," Woo-ri said with another slight grin. "I seem to make the same mistakes repeatedly."

"What mistakes have you made over and over?" I asked.

"I think I fall in love with the wrong people," Woo-ri shrugged. "Or maybe I fall in love for the wrong reasons. I don't know."

"What does *falling in love* mean to you?"

"What is that line from that famous movie?" Woo-ri said as she searched her brain for the answer. "Oh, it's 'you complete me!'" Woo-ri answered. "Love is finding someone who *completes* me. I don't feel whole, so I look for my other half, you know? I just want someone to make me feel lovable."

"How would your life be different if you found your 'other half,' as you said?" I asked, curious about what she might say, since I was just exploring this concept in my own life.

"I don't know," Woo-ri shrugged. "I don't think that person exists."

"What if the other half did exist," I asked, "and it was already inside of you?"

"What do you mean?" Woo-ri looked perplexed.

"I mean, what if you loved yourself in just the right way that you needed to be loved? How would you feel? What might your life look like?"

"I guess I'd stop looking for someone who's not there," Woo-ri shrugged as she tried picturing that kind of life. "I don't know, maybe I wouldn't be so critical of myself. I'd stop blaming myself for every bad thing that's happened in my life. I wouldn't listen to the voice in my head that tells me I'm not good enough."

"Whose voice do you hear?" I asked, sensing Woo-ri was ready to make a breakthrough. "Is it yours, or is it the voice of your parents?"

"I've never thought about whose voice it is," Woo-ri said after a moment. "But the words are those of my brother and parents."

"What if instead of using their words, you used words that told you of your worth? What if instead of criticizing or ignoring you, they affirmed you?" I asked.

"I see," Woo-ri said, nodding her head. "I could change what the voice tells me."

"Exactly," I said as she understood. "Start with this: What did you most want to hear as a child? And then move on to what you wish to hear now that you're an adult. We never outgrow the desire to be loved, encouraged, and supported."

"I don't know how to replace the voices in my head," Woo-ri shook her head.

"Start small," I suggested. "Instead of agreeing with the words that cross your mind, challenge any negative voice by saying something like, 'I am enough.' Do you think you can do that to start?"

"I am enough," Woo-ri repeated. "Yes, I can try that. Thank you. I am enough."

"So if a voice whispers in your head something like, 'I don't deserve to be happy,' or 'No one will ever love me,' shout back, 'I am enough.'"

"I can try that."

"Let's practice," I suggested. "Let's say that something happens that makes you remember a part of your childhood that made you feel unloved. And then maybe the words come to your head like, 'No one can love me. I'm unlovable.' What do you say?"

"I am enough!" Woo-ri said loudly with a smile.

"I love it!" I said encouragingly. "And can I tell you something?"

Woo-ri looked at me quizzically.

"I'm going to say, 'I am enough,' every time a voice in my head says something unkind to me too," I told her. "We will do this together. So let's do one more practice together. I'll count to three, and after I say 'three,' we'll both say it. Ready?"

Woo-ri nodded.

"One, two, three…" I counted, and then we said in unison, "I. Am. Enough!"

That might have been the best session I'd ever had with Woo-ri. I think I gave Woo-ri a useful tool. But I know I gave myself a gift by reminding myself that I, too, am enough.

Chapter Thirteen

"Never play another person's game. Play your own."
—Andrew Salter

"Haena showed up!" my mom told me in a breathless voice over the phone. "She showed up!"

Those wonderful words, uttered some seven thousand miles away, felt like a miracle.

"Tell me everything!" I said to my mom. "I will catch the soonest flight to South Korea that I can find!"

"No, no," my mom said, "Just wait. Let me tell you everything."

My mom told me that Haena just showed up at their door after all these years. Now an adult, she wanted to reconnect with family.

"She reached out to her dad, and we're waiting to see how that goes," my mom explained. "I know you've had problems with Young Suk in the past," Mom started to say.

"And so have you," I reminded her. "He's the reason you're in debt and in assisted living, hiding from the mafia."

"Yes, yes," she said, "that's true. But I don't want Haena to hear these negative things about her father from you or us. She should get to know him without having already made up her mind about him because of what other people say about him."

"I don't have to say anything about Young Suk," I said quickly. "He wouldn't even have to know that I was in South Korea. But I'm Haena's aunt, and I've been wanting to meet her since I heard she existed!"

"Yes, I know, Heawon," Mom said rationally. "We have another reason for you to wait. We don't know if maybe she and her mother have some ulterior motive for reaching out to us. What if they want money? We would like to wait before we open all of our lives to her, just until we know more."

"I'm still coming," I told my mom, no longer asking permission.

"OK, fine. Come out. We'd love to see you. But please don't try to meet her when you're here. Just let her reconnect with her father, and then we'll see what happens from there. It will take time to know if she wants a relationship with us all, or if she wants something else."

I flew out on a Sunday and returned the next Sunday. I had many clients, and I knew that some of them would struggle if I were gone for any longer than that.

The family reunited in South Korea. One big, happy family. Except for me. My parents learned that Young Suk worked as a cab driver and lived in a one-room rooming house in Suwon where their assisted living complex was located. Apparently, he still drank, but somehow managed to support himself. My parents didn't want me around Haena or Haena's mother. And I didn't want to see my brother. I had to rely on information about Haena from what my parents told me.

"Haena asked about you," my mother told me.

"Really? What did she want to know?"

"'Where is my aunt? I heard she lives in America. Can I contact her?'" my mom relayed.

"Of course she can!" I said excitedly.

"Well, I told her no," Mom shook her head.

"What? Why would you do that? I came all the way to South Korea because of her, and now I can't even contact her?"

"Well, we told her, 'Your aunt is not the kind of person you want to know. She's one of the most selfish people you'll ever meet.' We told her that to protect you," my mom explained while I looked at her, stunned.

"From what? Why would you do that?!" I demanded.

"We said that in order to keep Haena from looking for you," Mom answered. "Haena told us that her stepfather has been abusive to her, preferring his child from his previous marriage. That is why she wanted to find her biological father. Remember, we want her to bond with her father for now. And we want to know if she and her mother are trying to take advantage of all of us."

"Can you at least give me her address so I can write to her?" I asked, hoping for a crumb from my parents.

"Just wait," Mom answered. "Give it time."

I returned to New York defeated. I didn't know what to believe. I'd hoped that I was starting to build a relationship with my parents, but I came to understand that wasn't true. As soon as Young Suk came back into their lives, he took center stage, and I became invisible, unwanted. And then they lied to my niece to keep her from ever wanting to know me!

Still, I'd come to accept that events happen in our lives for different reasons. No matter what occurred, I'd always try to assign meaning to each experience, so I could use it to propel me forward.

After walking through a few days in a haze from sadness and fatigue after my long flights, I found a purpose in this situation. Back in college, my best friend and I talked about opening a house for young kids to come talk to us and have a safe place. Realizing that I couldn't do anything to meet Haena or be in her life at this time, I started to rekindle this idea.

Maybe that's what I should focus on now. I can love other children just the way I wished I could love my own niece that I don't know, I thought. While visiting with my parents in South Korea, they told me that Haena had become the odd one of the family. Her mother remarried, and her stepfather abused her. *If I can't help my blood, I will help the next person who needs me.*

I began to organize community resources in Suffolk County where I now lived. I focused much time on places like universities and other social agencies that worked with young adults who would have been close to Haena's age. Then, from my years in social services, I called in favors and tapped into like-minded individuals to donate their time as mentors to young adults in need.

I started working with universities, libraries, and social work departments to hire social work students to do community work. I realized that I didn't need to rent office space for my programs if I tapped into the local libraries in Suffolk County. The program brought systemic change across the county. Universities could now place their social work students as interns to work in the libraries where they'd serve community residents.

In addition to doing my full-time job, I recruited people to join the cause and spoke to any group that had resources and was willing to listen. Before long, I felt like I had two full-time jobs. I juggled my personal clients and this outreach with the help of other supportive volunteers.

After three years of helping New York's Haenas, I reached out to my parents to ask once more if I could have Haena's contact information.

"No," my father said. "It's still too soon."

"I think three years is more than enough time for her to get to know her father," I argued. "She obviously doesn't have any ulterior motive. And if she tried to take advantage of me, I'm a big girl. I can take care of myself."

"Well, three years is not long enough. Your brother thinks Haena may visit him, so we had to help him get a one-bedroom apartment so she would have a place to sleep. We also had to help him with his dental implants because he doesn't want to look bad in front of his daughter. So we are still watching to see how their relationship develops," my father argued back. "Why don't we wait and see what the situation looks like in another five years?"

That's when I realized they had no intention of ever giving me Haena's contact information. If I wanted to get to know Haena, it fell to me. My family hadn't changed. My brother knew how to manipulate them to pay for things for him, and they gladly did that while asking me to help them financially.

I started searching for records of Haena in Oregon, in the United States, where my parents said she lived, but I had no idea how to find her. At one point, my father had said that he thought she was attending a college and studying accounting. So I posted her photo on Facebook asking if anybody recognized her. Nothing. I contacted friends who knew people in Oregon, so that they could distribute the photo. Nothing. I tried Ancestry.com and contacted detectives, but I still got no results. I even considered reaching out to Howie Mandel who had TV programs where he worked to locate long-lost family members.

In the meantime, I repeatedly asked my parents for Heana's contact information, but they refused. Finally, I told them the only way I would continue to have a relationship with them would be for them to connect me to Haena. They still wouldn't give me her information.

Why do I have such self-deluding optimism when it comes to my parents? I chided myself. *No matter how they've treated me throughout my life, I forever become willing to forgive them and let them back into my heart.*

For all the work I'd done on my inner child, the helpless, scared little girl in me somehow remained hopeful that my parents would someday wake up and start loving me. But both my mother and father were extreme narcissists, and neither seemed to understand or care about the emotional needs of their children or their only granddaughter.

Instead, my father lived for the admiration of his students, peers, and fellow countrymen. So of course, he relished when others called him the Korean Freud. But my father had almost nothing to do with Sigmund Freud, who was an Austrian neurologist and the founder of psychotherapy. He delved into the psyches of clients to help resolve underlying pathologies. Freud understood both the workings of the mind as well as human emotions and behaviors. Freud's daughter, Anna, followed in her famous father psychologist's footsteps. Father and daughter didn't always agree with one another. But here's the thing: they always respected the insights the other developed.

I'd followed in my famous father's footsteps too. Not because I admired him, but because I wanted to help others who were suffering like me. And unlike Sigmund and his daughter, Anna, my father never respected or valued me as a person or as a professional.

My mother's narcissism looked a little different. While she also thought too highly of herself, her narcissism came out most in the way that she tried to keep me down so she could seem superior in comparison. Whenever anyone would praise my artwork, piano playing, grades, or singing, she would knock me down.

"Her? She is not talented," my mother would say. "She does her best, I suppose, but she is so ugly! I told her that she needed plastic surgery, but she refuses."

Young Suk, though, escaped the blistering criticism and abuse from my parents for a couple of reasons. One, he was very intelligent, which my father respected. Of course, my father attributed Young Suk's intelligence to the superior genes he contributed. Having such a bright son made my father look and feel good about himself.

Two, I think Young Suk scared them. From around age ten, an impenetrable darkness fell over Young Suk. He grew increasingly cruel and selfish. He'd been thrown out of schools for his behavior towards others, and he brought the police to our door more than once. And he beat me regularly and even abused my mom.

For my parents to acknowledge that there was something wrong with Young Suk would have been a bad reflection on them. Through the years, I'd pleaded with my parents to get help for my brother, and they had dismissed me each time.

From third grade until today, I experience fainting spells and panic attacks because of my brother's abuse. *But no, Young Suk is fine. There's nothing wrong with him.*

No more. My seemingly limitless patience with my parents ran out. The time had come for me to move on emotionally, just as I'd done physically years earlier.

Chapter Fourteen

*"I can be changed by what happens to me.
But I refuse to be reduced by it."*
—Maya Angelou

I threw myself into my nonprofit organization with new energy. The mentor-mentee program couldn't happen without the committed group of volunteers that stepped forward. They were a giving bunch of people, mostly older, and financially well-off. They were looking for meaning in their lives, especially for those who were retired and had more time on their hands.

The mentors attended monthly trainings, given by me, and provided their time selflessly to guide young adults in their twenties by making their futures brighter. These adults were hungry to absorb the wisdom from the more experienced mentors, and they benefited from the emotional support and practical advice their mentors offered. While I saw the program's efficacy, I grew troubled when I saw mentors starting to leave the program. A few of them had personal situations arise, which I understood. But most seemed to leave when the program didn't offer exactly what they expected. That was a surprise to me.

As I thought about it, I acknowledged that I tended to hold on to my commitments tightly, maybe even a little more tightly than was healthy for me. I chalked that up to my struggles with self-esteem and grandiosity. But I stuck to most of my commitments because of my perseverance and resilience. When mentors started leaving the program, I wondered if I had the discernment to know if I held on to the program because of my low self-esteem or my resilience.

This question led me to an internal dialogue about the patterns of my life.

I thought back to my upbringing. Like all children, I wanted unconditional love, support, encouragement, and guidance. But I learned early on that I should never expect those things. When I received a small dose of any of those elements, I savored the moments and appreciated them. When I realized that they wouldn't last, I felt heartbroken. Early on, I decided I wasn't going to inflict that kind of pain on others.

In my childhood, music became my salvation—and escape from turmoil. No matter what was going on at home, I looked forward to music class at school. On the days I felt too broken to sing, I played a pipe.

I'll never forget the day I walked home from school. I'd had a rough several weeks from my brother's abuse, and I feared being at home more than even the most crime-ridden areas in town. As I took a meandering route home, I heard a tune coming from a house. Its tone melded both sorrow and joy, and as such, it made my heart break and soar simultaneously.

Years later, I learned the tune was called "Für Elise" by Beethoven.

My heart was full of desire to play the piano and make beautiful music like I'd heard coming out of that house. Since I didn't have a piano at home, I volunteered to clean the music room at school to get access to a piano. While other students viewed cleaning a room in the school as a chore, I saw it as a blessing. The teacher gave me a key to the music room so I could clean around my schedule. This key gave me access to two critical things: a piano to play, and a safe place to escape.

And I frequently needed an escape from home. I didn't sleep well at night, because I was too afraid that my brother would come in to hurt me while I slept. One morning after my brother abused me in the night, I left the house at 5:00 a.m. and walked to school. Because I held the key to the music room, I could get into the school whenever I needed to get away.

I'll be safe here, I told myself as I opened my textbooks to study in the music room. At some point, I got ink on my hands. Since the music room had a sink in the corner, I washed my hands.

At the time, a teacher would stay in the school overnight on rotation, just to make sure that no one broke into the school. That night, the science teacher took his turn on school watch. Alarmed by a sound in the music room, he came to check out the source. I had my back turned to him. He saw me, but I couldn't see him. He came up behind me at the sink, and then he kissed me on my cheek. I jumped, and then he jumped before quickly leaving the room.

I was twelve years old. I didn't know much about life, but I knew that what happened was not normal or appropriate. His kiss hadn't been a "oh-bless-your-heart-for-getting-to-school-so-early-to-study-my-poor-child" kiss. I didn't pretend to know what was going on, but I knew enough to be concerned.

Later at home, I wrote about that situation in my diary. Whenever something happened that I didn't understand, I'd write it down so I could look for an answer.

Unfortunately, unbeknownst to me, my mother regularly found and read my diary. When I returned home the next day after school, my mother and father were waiting for me.

"Stand here!" my father commanded me. I complied, dropping my eyes to focus on the long, heavy stick my father held in his hand.

"What happened with your science teacher?" he asked.

"I, uh," I stammered. Embarrassed, I didn't know what to say. After all, I didn't even understand what had happened with the science teacher either. So I said nothing.

Whack! My father brought the stick down on the bones at the top of my feet.

"What happened?" he yelled again.

"I," I stared, and still had no words.

Whack! Whack, whack, whack! Each hit from the thick, heavy stick felt like it crushed my little bones.

"Stop! Please, stop! I don't know what happened!" I wailed in both humiliation and tremendous pain. "Just what I wrote in my diary! He kissed my cheek and left."

And then the beating stopped. As did the conversation. It was as if they beat me and forced me to recount my traumatic experience so they could add more pain and humiliation to my brokenness. They never contacted the school. They never reached out to the teacher. They never spoke of it again, just like the time my mother pushed my father to kiss me.

This situation proved that my father, the Korean Freud, knew nothing about parenting. Any nurturing instincts he possessed, he offered to his college students; any insights he had, he applied them to writing social policies. He focused his energy championing the societal welfare of children and families in South Korea. Whenever I heard my father speaking with his colleagues about cruelty to children and the importance of prevention, I would scream on the inside, *You're a two-faced hypocrite, Dad!*

The day before I snuck off to the school had started with my brother abusing me. Then my science teacher kissed my cheek, crossing a line that would later land a teacher in prison, or at the very least, lead to getting fired from teaching. And then my father beat me instead of equipping me to deal with unwanted attention.

I knew I'd done nothing wrong, yet I didn't have a path to justice. The only way out of this madness was through studying.

That will lead me to my freedom and salvation, I told myself. So I kept my focus on studying.

My love of music brought me to church, with choirs full of unskilled musicians creating tones that could have been a chorus of angels, at least to my ears. Wanting to invest in something that brought me pure joy, as a high school junior, I became the pianist for the children's choir at my church. The choir teacher, a brilliant college student, played the guitar, loved classical literature, and taught Bible school.

Knowing my love of music, he came to me after practice one night.

"Come on, Heawon," my *seonsaengnim* (Korean word for teacher), said with an eager smile. "I want you to hear something." He brought me into a room full of headphones, and he placed a set over my ears. "Listen to this," he smiled.

For the next couple of hours, he played one classical composer after another: Bach, Mozart, Beethoven. My heart soared as I again heard "Für Elise"! He introduced me to other long-deceased composers who wrote such heavenly music that it must have been inspired by God. The melodies spoke directly to my soul, and they took me to a magical world.

"Thank you, *seonsaengnim*," I said. "That music moved my spirit."

Later, my teacher had another surprise for me.

"Hey, Heawon," he said with a slight tilt of his head. "What are you doing tomorrow?"

"I'm going to school," I said with a laugh. "It's a school day."

"What do you think about playing hooky with me?" he asked. "I want to show you something I think you'll like."

He'd opened me up to a new world of music. I could only imagine what sort of enchantment he could show me if I played hooky with him. As much as I loved school, I couldn't say no. I needed to know what new world he might show me.

"What do you have in mind?" I asked, hoping to get a hint.

"I'd like to take you on a train ride out of the city," he said, meaning somewhere outside of Seoul.

The next day, I could hardly contain my excitement. After I met him at the train station, we found a seat and settled in for the trip. Along the way, we talked about classic literature, philosophy, and religion. Whenever I met someone who had read the same books I'd read, I loved discussing what I'd learned and asking questions so I could learn even more. And he had great depth on many topics. I wished the train ride would keep going.

Once the train stopped, we got out. Looking around, I couldn't imagine what he could show me there. We were surrounded by farmland and rice fields.

"Come on," he said, taking my hand.

At the time, I figured he took my hand because we were walking through a rutted, nearly-sown field.

Within minutes, the few homes scattered near the train shrank in the distance. After walking another fifteen minutes, he stopped.

"Please, sit down," he said, gesturing to the ground.

Before I sat, I looked around. In every direction, all I could see was a vast, flat field.

"OK," I said agreeably but a little confused.

He sat next to me, and we spent a few minutes in silence. Then we lay back on the ground and looked up at the clouds moving slowly overhead. I could hear a few insects and birds in the distance.

Then he rolled over and tried to kiss me.

"Wait!" I said. "Please stop."

He gave me a quizzical look for a moment, and then he reached over and tried to fondle me.

"No!" I said, standing up. "This is what you wanted to *show* me, *seonsaengnim*?" I asked sarcastically.

I stormed back the way we'd come, boarded the next train back to Seoul, and returned home, disappointed and disillusioned. I'd met someone smart, musical, and interesting, but all he wanted to do was objectify me sexually. I enjoyed the months I'd spent getting to know him, but I stopped attending that church so I wouldn't have to see him again.

Still, I savored what I'd learned about enchanting classical music and kept studying.

In high school, I had a two-and-a-half-hour commute to and from school each day. As part of that commute, I needed to switch buses three times each way. In bad weather, my commute could take seven hours.

My senior year, my homeroom teacher created a twisted rule: "If you're late once, you will receive one hundred strikes with this." He held up a long, two-inch thick slab of wood. "You will receive one hundred more hits at the end of the week, and another one hundred hits at the end of the month."

Our classroom of students listened wide-eyed as he issued his warning. But he wasn't finished.

"Should any student arrive late *twice* in one month, instead of one hundred strikes, the number goes up to *two hundred*," he announced as coldly, as if he were describing what he'd do to a sheet of paper.

Because of bad weather, my buses ran late one day. I arrived in his class five minutes late. I survived the hundred whacks that day and at the end of the week. But when he hit me at the end of the month, he broke my hand.

This was the world I grew up in, the only world I knew until I moved to the US.

I'd never considered myself a quick learner, so I chose the turtle as my spirit animal. I fantasized that, like the turtle, I would eventually win the race. While some students could read a math or English textbook once and understand everything they read, I often used three or four reference books to look up words and concepts that I didn't understand. Additionally, after regular school, I went to a special academy that provided extra tutelage in math and English, my two hardest subjects. To cram in school, the after-school tutorials at the academy, and my long commute, I'd leave my home at 5:30 a.m. and wouldn't return home until 11:00 p.m. I slept one or two hours each night, and I spent the rest of the time studying so I could excel in school.

But even with such long days, I often took an earlier bus in the morning, so I could get off at a stop that was a ten-minute walk from my new church. I'd walk to the sanctuary and pray for a half-hour before walking back to the bus stop and continuing my commute. Music and God were my sunshine, my simple joys. I always made time for those two parts of my life.

Anyone driving by would have wondered about the tiny girl carrying three big bags, standing in the rain, waiting for a bus. We didn't have lockers at school, so I had to carry my textbooks, class notebooks, and reference books with me throughout the day. When I had art or gym, I'd have to carry art supplies or gym clothes as well. I had no room to carry lunch, and our school didn't have a cafeteria. Throughout my three years in high school, I went without breakfast or lunch. Dinner served as my one and only meal each day.

One winter morning, I got off at the stop so I could walk to church. There are few homes in the area, and it must have been a very cloudy morning. Everything looked pitch-black around me. I headed in the direction I believed to be the church, but I couldn't be sure.

Then, while I continued to walk, several small, yellow lights danced around me. I'd never seen anything like that before or since. Had this been the summer, and had I been in a very narrow section of one corner of South Korea, they might have been fireflies. But it was winter, and lightning bugs are rare in South Korea. The lights terrified me. *Are these ghosts?* I wondered.

I stopped to pray. "God, please help me. Help me get to the church safely."

Korean churches have little red crosses on top. But these lights are very dim, like small LED lights that don't throw off much brightness. Suddenly, while I prayed, I saw the dim red cross in front of me. But the cross wasn't dim any longer. It shone brightly, like a spotlight that hits the podium of the Academy Awards' stage. And that beam of light stayed on me until I arrived at the church.

"Thank you for hearing my prayer, God," I said aloud as I stepped inside the sanctuary.

After Asper and I broke up, I spent more time at the church I'd been attending. Within one month's time, all three pastors of my church made sexual overtures towards me.

While attending a Bible study at one of the pastor's homes, the pastor pulled me out into the hallway when his wife went into the kitchen for something.

"Hey, Heawon," he said in a low voice. "I want to tell you something. When is a good day for me to come to your house?"

"What do you mean?" I asked, feeling like I'd missed half of the conversation. "We have Bible teachings in your home and at church."

"No, no, no," he shook his head. "I have something to tell you, and I don't want anybody to hear what I have to say to you."

You have something to tell me that you don't want anybody to hear? Gee, I wonder what could that be? I thought as I shook my head no.

"No, I don't like that idea," I said and rejoined the others. For the rest of the night, I avoided eye contact with him. A couple more times, he tried to approach me, and I cut him off each time.

A week later, another junior pastor showed up at my door.

"Hi, Heawon," he said with a smile. "I just wanted to see how you were doing. I know Asper's gone, so I wanted to see if you needed anything."

"Thank you," I said. "That's kind of you. Would you like to come in for some tea?"

"Sure, sure," he said as he entered the house.

Moments after I brought him some hot tea, he slid over next to me on the couch and tried to kiss me.

"No," I said, standing up quickly. "Get out!"

A couple of weeks later, the head pastor waved me down after the Sunday evening services.

"Would you be willing to stay until the others have gone?" he asks.

Here we go again, I thought. *There is no wholesome, valid reason why he wants me to stay after everyone else has exited the building.*

"I'm sorry, no," I said as I waved and walked away.

My whole life felt like one connection after another with people and events that seemed to offer me something beneficial and real. Then things would turn, and I would be disappointed. Each painful experience from my brother, parents, teachers, pastors, friends, and acquaintances would test me. I learned to savor the parts that brought goodness into my life, and then I would move on. Isn't that what bees do with flowers? After they get nectar from the flower, they move on to the next. While doing that, they also pollinate—and create honey!

I didn't create this "honey"—in the form of resilience and perseverance—in the absence of struggles. Anyone can be strong in pleasant, easy times. But to become resilient, I needed to face enough storms and survive.

My parents' neglect forced me to build resilience. My brother's abuse pounded me against the forge of my parents' coldness, turning me into a fiercely strong, optimistic woman. So I pressed on like I had each time in my life. As I thought about how I'd gotten to this moment, I knew what I needed to do. I thanked the volunteers for their work. Then I shifted my focus slightly not only to directly serve the community by counseling clients, but also to mentor other social workers so we could expand our reach. In my mind, the nonprofit became a "counseling depot."

At the same time, I continued providing my community-based psychotherapy for those in need.

I still hadn't located Haena. But I kept doing my best, including coming to the aid of the Haenas in Suffolk County. And for now, that would need to be enough.

Chapter Fifteen

"The sorrow was no less in reality, but it became less oppressive from having someone in precisely the same relation to it as that in which she stood."
—Elizabeth Gaskell, *North and South*

I'd been in my new house for a couple of years, worked full time in my private practice, kept my foundation going, and continued to look for Haena. While I'd gotten into a strong routine, that changed when I lost my sweet Cosmo and three close friends suddenly. I withdrew inwardly to process my grief, and I stopped going out except for work as a natural reflex to the losses.

"I'm here if you want to talk about it," a colleague offered. A friend told me, "It's not good to be alone at a time like this. You need to stay around people who love you."

I appreciated those who offered advice and comfort, but I told myself, *Nobody knows me like I do*. Some people want to be alone when they are sick, while others want to be tended to constantly. Neither is right or wrong. It just depends on the person's preference. And when I'm sick, I want to be left alone, which was precisely what I needed to mend my broken heart. I listened to my body and the soft whispers calling me to mourn deeply, personally, and respectfully.

My whole being mourned the loss of Cosmo, my faithful best friend and reincarnated soul of Paduki, the one who shared every shadow that crossed our valleys and each heavenly light that shined on our mountaintops. Then I slowly processed the loss of my close friends, whose voices had fallen silent, whose warmth had suddenly turned cold, and whose light had been extinguished so suddenly.

When we grieve the death of ones we have loved, our hearts and minds stir with multiple emotions. We have gratitude that we knew and loved them, but we mourn for our separation from them. We also delight for them, knowing that they feel no pain after they transition from life to the beyond, yet we weep for ourselves, feeling like a part of ourselves has gone with them. Finally, we recognize our own future passage, not knowing if it approaches at a close or distant time. And we wonder what our own loved ones will say and feel when we leave them behind.

While I remained entombed in private mourning, the world continued to spin, indifferent to my grief. Thankfully, at work, my heart remained open, and as Thursday at 4:00 p.m. approached, I found myself looking forward to my meeting with Woo-ri.

"Hello Woo-ri, please come in," I said with deep affection.

"Thank you, my sweet friend," Woo-ri said kindly.

"I'd love for you to catch me up on what's new and how things have been going for you," I said.

"Well," Woo-ri started, her eyes drifting out the window. She said nothing more for a few moments while I sat patiently.

"Do you remember my first visit with you?" she asked at last.

"Yes," I nodded. "I remember it quite well. You told me about a recurring nightmare you had about the earthquake on your honeymoon. Has the nightmare returned?"

"No," Woo-ri answered with a short word.

"I'm glad to hear that," I responded, waiting for her to say more.

Woo-ri shifted sideways in her seat with her back against the armrest of the couch, and she drew her legs up to her chest while wrapping her arms around her knees. I recognized the protective position she took whenever she had something troubling that she didn't know how to say.

I waited.

"At our first meeting, I told you that I didn't think you could help me," she said, her gaze still in another world. "Do you remember?"

"Yes, I remember," I said with a nod.

"Before I started opening up to you, I didn't fully realize just how much my childhood experiences affected me. I knew my past stayed with me, but I've come to see that some events in my life have changed the way I see myself and my place in the world. You offered me safety, and I've been able to tell you some things that I've never shared with anyone." She paused, as if to let me respond.

"I'm so glad you've gained some valuable insight about yourself, Woo-ri," I replied. "That's what I hoped the two of us could accomplish together. I get a sense that you have other things that you'd like to share," I added, opening the door for her to say more.

"You're so wise," Woo-ri smiled nervously. "It's like you can read my mind…Yes, I do have more things I want to tell you, but I don't think I can."

"I think I understand your feelings, Woo-ri," I assured her. "Our room here and our moments together…I want you to see this as our sanctuary, a place where nothing bad can happen. That might not make you feel completely safe, but I want to assure you that nothing you say or do will damage the nature of our friendship or threaten your safety."

Then I simply waited to see if she felt comfortable enough to share more. I watched as Woo-ri breathed shakily yet deeply through her nostrils, as if trying to soothe herself.

"My oppa" she spoke at last, still looking out the window. Then she slowly turned to me, holding my eyes for a moment before looking down at her hands on her lap.

"I hate him," she said, the muscles of her face tightening as she looked back at me.

"Can you say more about why you hate him?" I asked, not surprised at what she'd shared.

"He did terrible things to me," she said, her voice turning quieter as she looked own again.

"Woo-ri," I said soothingly, "your brother is not here. From what you've told me, he still lives in Korea and has no idea where you live or how to contact you. He can't reach you in here."

She nodded slightly in acknowledgment, keeping her eyes focused on a memory fixed in her past.

"I think you will feel better if you talk about it," I said. "You can let it out with screams, tears, and words, whatever. No harm can come to you in our room."

Woo-ri, who already seemed young for her age, went back in time as I watched. Her body transformed to that of a small child, and she pulled her body into a ball on the couch. She then began to sob quietly, her small shoulders shaking as she trembled.

An almost motherly instinct moved me. Getting up from my chair, I moved a box of tissues from the side table to her side while joining her on the sofa and wrapping my arm around her shoulders as she continued to weep. We stayed like that for several minutes, a therapist and a client.

Finally, she reached for a tissue and blew her nose, making a trumpet-like sound, breaking any final barrier that may have been between the two of us. We both let out a small nervous laugh. In Korea, blowing one's nose in public is considered rude. It's something you might do only in front of your closest loved ones.

"I'm sorry," Woo-ri said between laughter and tears.

"It's OK," I reassured her before repeating, "You're safe." I meant it. I hadn't felt remotely offended. Instead, I felt glad that she was comfortable enough not to censor something as innocuous as a nose-blowing.

Woo-ri regained her composure, and she sat rigidly against the side of the couch.

"It started when I was nine years old. Everything I did was wrong," Woo-ri said. "At least that's what he told me. He said that his job was to keep me from making so many mistakes, so each time I did something wrong, he would count my failings. And once I made three mistakes, he would punish me."

"How would he punish you?" I asked.

"He told me that he would have to 'examine' me to find out what was wrong with me," she said, her voice cracking. "Even as a small child, I knew he would do something bad to me. I didn't know what, but I believed it would be dreadful."

"You must have been very scared," I said, validating her feelings.

"But his counting was just part of a sick game," Woo-ri continued. "It didn't matter what I did, he would find something wrong with me. Like he would call me into the room where he was sitting. Then I would run to him quickly, not wishing to fail him. When I got there, he would say, 'You didn't bow' or 'You didn't move fast enough.' Then he would say, 'That's one.' I tried to be perfect, to do everything he asked of me. But he made sure that I always failed three times every day. And then..." her voice broke off, and she turned her head away from me and closed her eyes.

"What would he do after he told you that you had failed?" I asked, my heart racing while awaiting her reply.

Woo-ri sucked air loudly into her nose and blew it out slowly through her mouth.

"The first time he said, 'That's three,' he didn't get off the couch," Woo-ri said. "I felt so much relief, like maybe he'd just been trying to scare me. But a few hours later, he waited in the bathroom for me. I froze at the doorway and started to back away. But he said, 'Come here and close the door.' I was so scared."

"Then what happened?" I asked, pulling her through the story.

"I did as he commanded...He said, 'Take your pants down.' So I did. He looked at my private parts for a few minutes while I stood there with my eyes squeezed shut. Then he touched me," Woo-ri said at last, confirming what I had long expected.

I said nothing as I watched Woo-ri close her eyes tightly, her hands balled into fists on her lap. Finally, she continued, "And for the next several years, he would touch me nearly every day," she added.

"Where were your parents when he would touch you?" I asked, thinking about how my own parents often seemed unconcerned and disconnected from the trauma I experienced in my childhood.

"It didn't matter where my parents were. Oppa always found a way. If my parents were home, he would wait outside and take me to a nearby mountain. Or he would come into my bedroom during the night when my parents slept in the next room. He told me he would hurt me more if I locked my bedroom door."

"And your brother would do this each day?" I asked, absorbing the depth of her trauma.

"Yes, because I did so many bad things," Woo-ri sighed. "That's what he told me, and I couldn't avoid him. Even when I tried to be perfect, he would always catch me doing wrong things, like not opening my eyes wide enough or making a sound when I walked."

"Did you tell your parents about what was going on?" I asked, sickened as I pictured what this poor child had endured. I felt angry that her parents, like mine, had seemed absent.

"Not at first," Woo-ri said, shaking her head. "I was too afraid. After the first time he touched me, Oppa said that he would kill me if I ever told anyone. I believed him. And the humiliation? How could I talk about it or say anything to anyone?"

"Oh, Woo-ri," I said softly, rubbing her shoulder with my hand.

"But it never stopped. No matter what I did or where I'd go to get away from him, he'd find me," she said, now sobbing. "And when he'd touch me, I went to another place," she said, telling me how she had detached from her emotions and trauma.

Oh, my sweet, poor girl, my heart cried inside of me. *I understand this more than you know.*

"You went to another place in your head?" I asked for confirmation.

"Yes," she nodded. "I closed my eyes and waited until it was over." She thought for a moment before adding, "Have you ever dropped a flashlight, and the batteries fell out? That was me. When I saw my brother coming, I felt like someone pulled out my battery."

"You said you didn't tell your parents at first," I pushed deeper into her story. "But it sounds like you did tell them eventually?"

"Yes," Woo-ri said, her voice hardly above a whisper.

"And?" I asked to let her know I was staying with her in her story.

"Well, let me go back," Woo-ri said, shifting her posture on the couch to put her back against the cushion. "We'd eat dinner together most nights as a family, especially if my dad came home early enough. Sometimes Oppa stayed late after school, so he wasn't there. But whenever he joined us for dinner, I wouldn't eat much at all. I mostly pushed food around my plate, ate a couple of bites of rice and kimchi, or ate nothing at all. I wanted my parents to notice that I wasn't eating, that I was starving myself so they'd ask me if everything was OK. But they never noticed. Or if they noticed, they never said anything," her eyes flashed with anger and hurt as she remembered.

"One night when my brother wasn't at home, Dad mentioned that he'd be going away on a work project for a long time, and I panicked. I knew that if he left, my brother would become more vicious. So I begged my dad not to leave. 'Please, Dad! Don't leave me here! Please don't go away!' I pleaded with him. But he just laughed at me and told me to stop being silly."

I remembered having a very similar conversation with my own father when he planned to leave for Japan for his master's degree. And I recalled my own devastation when my plea went unanswered, as if my being abused didn't matter at all to him.

"I didn't know what else to do," Woo-ri said, her words coming faster as she relived the moment. "So finally, I blurted out, 'Oppa is touching my private parts, and I'm afraid of him! He told me he would kill me if I told you! That's why I don't want you to go away. He's hurting me, and I can't get away from him!"

Woo-ri's breathing slowed down, and she sat still.

After a long silence, I asked "What did your parents say?"

"My mom and dad looked at one another without saying anything. Then they looked at me. I wasn't sure if they'd heard me. Or I thought maybe they'd heard me but didn't believe me. Then my dad said, 'I will think about it.' That's all he said."

"I will think about *what*?" I leaned forward, picturing the woman in front of me as a small child confronting monstrous abuse to deaf parents.

"He would consider staying instead of leaving, I guess," she shrugged. "But he left anyway without saying anything to me about the abuse. And things got worse for me at home."

"How did they get worse?" I asked.

"I don't know if I can talk about this," Woo-ri said, her face vacillating between shame and rage. "Even after all the things I've told you, I can't bring myself to say what he did next."

A skilled therapist can meet with a new client, build trust, deconstruct years of unspeakable abuse, and celebrate their emotional healing with a hug after ninety minutes, at least according to the movies. But that's not how therapy works. Therapy is a relationship that takes time. By this time, I'd already met with Woo-ri for years, and it would take her more visits before she could slowly unwrap her secrets in her own time.

When I met with Woo-ri months later, I began by probing her readiness to share more.

"Do you think you can tell me parts about this thing that you're struggling to share? I don't need all the details, but maybe there are things you can say," I encouraged her.

"OK," she let out a long sigh. "I will try."

She shifted into a protective position on the sofa and found a spot on the wall behind me to lock her stare.

"One day, Oppa took me to a nearby mountain. The mountain scared me. Every tree cast a shadow of a monster. I couldn't feel the sun on my skin, and the roar of a nearby waterfall sounded like a steady groan."

"Anyway, Oppa led me to a cliff and then sat down, placing me between the edge of the cliff and himself. He sat so close that I could smell his sour breath, and I couldn't see the mountains behind him. Then he pulled a knife from his pocket and set it by his side," Woo-ri said, returning to the moment.

"'Nothing will happen to you,' he said, '*if* you do what I tell you. But if you don't obey me,' he said as he picked up his knife, 'I will cut you until you listen.' He said this with no emotion. He didn't seem angry or happy, which made me even more scared. Then he told me what he wanted me to do…" Woo-ri said, turning her face further from me. "What he told me to do was so much more humiliating than all the things he had done so far. And I hesitated. I told myself, *I just should jump off the cliff to end this. I practiced dying my entire life. I shouldn't be afraid because he can no longer hurt me if I'm dead.* When I didn't move, he stood up with the knife in his hand. As he raised his arm with the knife, I did what he told me to do before I could stop myself," Woo-ri said, weeping so deeply that her body trembled.

I immediately moved next to her and held her gently until her body went limp.

After sitting like this for several minutes, Woo-ri continued with rage in her voice, even as her tears continued. "I was so mad at myself! I wanted to jump but didn't. I didn't have the courage," Woo-ri wailed as she saw the scene in her head and felt a wave of despair for choosing to live instead of just dying.

"Woo-ri," I responded with empathy. "I am so sorry that you went through such horror by the hand of your own brother, someone who should have protected you, not hurt you. Do you know what? You *do* have courage. To go on living despite trauma takes a different type of courage. And do you know what else? The shame belongs to your oppa, not you…The shame is not yours, Woo-ri, it is your oppa's," I repeated softly, several times.

Then I stopped speaking and rocked her gently.

After several minutes passed, Woo-ri said in a tiny, childlike voice, "It is not my shame. It belongs to Oppa." She said this so quietly that I barely heard it, yet I knew what I'd heard.

Finally, she straightened herself and wiped away her tears. I could see her shifting from raw emotion to trying to think clearly.

"How can I forgive myself for living? I know what you mean when you say that the shame belongs to him," she explained. "Yet I still think it would have been better if I'd had the courage to die. I remember finding a book in my brother's room later. It was about German experiments on Jews under Hitler's order. Oppa studied ways to experiment on me to see how I would react under his terror. Physical abuse made me feel powerless but didn't remove my dignity. His previous sexual abuse had humiliated me and filled me with shame, but I still had my humanity. But after what he did that day, I lost it all. I was a rat in his laboratory," Woo-ri moaned.

When I didn't think my heart could break any more for her, I felt it splinter further.

"Do you know any young girl, one who's about nine years old?" I asked, thinking about Miguel's nine-year-old niece.

Woo-ri answered immediately. "Yes, I have a niece that age."

"Would you think that way if your niece told you the same

thing...if she experienced something like what you went through? Would you tell her that she was a coward for not jumping to her death and taking her own life?"

"Never!" Woo-ri emphatically shook her head.

I waved a hand in Woo-ri's direction as a gesture to mean, *Why would you not believe yourself just as worthy to keep living?*

"Will the pain go away?" Woo-ri asked, relaxing her body and stretching her legs out until her feet again touched the floor.

"Yes, the pain fades with time," I said, wiping my eyes, "but you will never forget it. Trauma scorched your soul, leaving nerves exposed. You will live with your triggers, when you feel like they are opening new wounds. But they aren't new. They are from your childhood. And do you know what I've recently discovered? Pain can make people strong. It's a matter of choice. Some people become villains themselves, and some, like you, become caring people. I've also heard that the best revenge is to live well. You have done that, Woo-ri. You are living such a full life, achieving all of your dreams."

If anyone had the ability to see through the walls and into our meeting room, they wouldn't have known what to make of the sight of me holding myself tightly and rocking gently side to side while tears rolled down my cheeks.

Chapter Sixteen

*"It is frightening when a woman finally realizes
that there is no answer to the question 'Who am I'
except the voice inside herself."*
—Betty Friedan

"Woo-ri Heawon!" Margherita greeted me warmly at her front door when I arrived at her place. "There's my girl!" she squealed as she gave me a tight hug. "I can't tell you how much I've missed you!"

In the years since I'd seen her last, Margherita had moved to Florida. Sadly, I learned that she was showing signs of early dementia. But I found myself grateful that I could visit her in Florida while some mental acuity remained. Gone were the sumptuous meals she used to make. Now she could offer me a market-bought salad fresh from her refrigerator.

After opening a bottle of wine, we picked at our meal while catching up with each other's lives. I told her about my flourishing practice and mentoring program as well as my ongoing search for Haena. Margherita told me about her separation from David, who had been her life partner for twenty years. But she had a constant source of happiness: her youngest daughter lived two blocks away. She told me that her daughter's presence was a godsend, since she occasionally got lost and needed help finding her way back home. Margherita's willingness to be open about her condition and make me her honored confidante humbled me.

While clearing the dinner table, she asked, "Hey, I meant to ask you. How have the sessions between Woo-ri and Heawon been going?

I wondered if she would remember that she'd asked me years earlier to spend time with my inner child.

She remembered.

Smiling, I responded, "You'll be happy to know that we've spent time faithfully since we came up with the name Woo-ri. Remember? You loved the name, because it sounded to you like I said 'worry,' and I loved it because in Korean, Woo-ri means *our*. Anyway, throughout the years, we've had many in-depth, productive sessions where we reached many breakthroughs together. Woo-ri trusts me to know that I will always care for, love, and protect her until the end."

"I'm so glad! Would you do the honor of cutting us some cake? It's a banana pudding cake I got from the bakery, and I'm dying to try it," Margherita asked while she busied herself making coffee. "And I'm not on a diet, so don't be stingy on my piece!" she added with a laugh. "That's another thing I enjoy about being single. I can eat whatever I want!" she said with another laugh.

As I cut into the cake, I let the fragrance of the bananas fill my nostrils, and it transported me back to my childhood when I'd eaten my first banana. It had been a forbidden fruit, but Woo-ri—now fully integrated into my own psyche—had snuck one out of the kitchen when "our" mom wasn't looking. Of course, it got me locked in the basement for hours, but I never blamed the banana. I still loved the smell and taste of them after all these years.

Once Margherita filled our coffee cups, she returned to the table. "You don't have to share any details, but what did you learn in your meetings with Woo-ri?" Margherita asked me before taking a bite.

"First, I must tell you how delicious this cake is, Margherita! I've never had a banana pudding cake before! I'm going back to that bakery tomorrow!" Then I took some time to consider. "Well, let me see. What did I learn from Woo-ri? I think my number one takeaway is that I am *OK*. When I say *OK*, I mean I've discovered radical self-acceptance. I've learned to love and accept myself, warts and all. I think about little Woo-ri as a baby and can't help but love her the way she was. It has taken years to see her as beautiful and perfect just as she was."

"I'm glad you've come to realize how beautiful and perfect you are, Heawon," Margherita nodded. "And I'm ecstatic that you've come to love yourself too. In my mind, that's the biggest challenge humans face."

"Thank you," I answered sincerely. "It's funny, I've always been *OK* to a point, but I never really felt *OK*, if that makes sense. My mom rejected me because I was ugly with my 'too dark' skin. My father ignored me because he got more gratification from students and politicians worshipping him than from being a decent dad. My brother hated me because he saw a strength in me that threatened him, so he repeatedly tried to break me. Some members of society rejected me because I didn't adhere to their specific ideology. Certain men rejected me because I resisted being objectified. But I finally realized that I don't need anyone else's approval. I just need to approve of myself."

"It's hard to let go of something that's always been part of us, isn't it?" Margherita asked tenderly.

"Yes, but the fear that had owned me didn't serve me. I've learned that the shame I've lived with was never mine to begin with. It didn't belong to me, so I let it go," I told her before sipping my coffee.

"You make it sound so simple." Margherita smiled at me. "But I know it wasn't easy."

"No, it was terrifying," I nodded. "You know all the defense mechanisms clients put up to feel safe. I tried them all. But at the same time, I wanted to learn and grow, to challenge myself, and to be free. I began analyzing myself, pulling up pieces of my past to see what they could teach me about myself. But life doesn't stop just because we need to heal! I had to deal with a failed relationship, loneliness, self-criticism, self-sabotage, grief, new projects, and losses. For a while, I didn't know who I was without the weight of shame. I repeatedly put myself on that cliff and jumped off. Figuratively, of course.

"I did this when I first came to the country knowing nothing," I continued. "Then before I knew it, I got put in charge of three hundred mentally ill patients each weekend, as the only mental health counselor on duty where violence was routine. It's like I kept going up to the hotel room to sleep while an earthquake raged below. I slept, but my mind never rested. Finally, I realized that I didn't need to do that anymore to prove that I had the right to live, to be accepted, or to be loved. As I started to let go—just a little at first—I began to feel liberated. And today, I feel like a free spirit and a free woman. But it's taken me years to get rid of the shame I've carried."

"I'm so happy for you, *Woo-ri Heawon*," Margherita said, squeezing my hand across the table. "Almost any therapist can treat others, but it takes a truly gifted one to help herself."

"Thank you for pushing me to face my past," I told Margherita as I squeezed her hand back with both of my own. "I'm not the same person I was when I first met you."

"You know what else?" I went on. "I think we therapists have taught clients concepts that are no longer suitable...like forgiveness, for example. I'd always been taught that I needed to forgive before I could heal completely. But I don't think that's true. It seems unwise to forgive people who continue to hurt you. While I don't dwell on the hurt, I don't waste time trying to forgive the villain to feel free and complete. There's a saying, *let go and let*

God. Who am I to judge the fate of someone who tormented me, to deem them forgivable or unforgivable? I see a lot of clients who feel shame for not being able to forgive. It's more damaging to have those kinds of expectations or demands for those who have lived through trauma."

"You're right," Margherita nodded. "I spent so much time trying to get my clients to forgive their abusers. I wonder if that approach made them feel revictimized, like the reason they couldn't heal was because they couldn't forgive."

"Exactly," I said excitedly, so grateful that my dear friend's mind seemed as clear as the last time we spoke. "And tied to forgiveness, don't you remember clients suffering from inappropriate guilt? Like those who live in guilt, telling themselves, 'I should do this,' or 'I should do that,' even when they know that guilt is a wasted emotion. Society puts so many *shoulds* on us that it's hard to think and live freely. Everyone wants to live authentically, but then many of us live out of guilt instead of love. I want to do things out of love."

Margherita nodded her head in acknowledgment and then said, "I'm so proud of you, sweetie. You're all grown up now, and you're thinking for yourself instead of living out your past. There really don't need to be so many absolutes when it comes to therapy and counseling modalities. Society changes, and we need to change with it. If trying to love and forgive your abusive parents rips you apart and keeps you in pain, release them from your life. The pain will leave too. We each make our own choices and must be willing to live with the consequences, right?"

"Right!" I affirmed.

Before I left Margherita, we hugged each other closely as I stood at the door.

That was the last time I saw her before she passed away.

Epilogue

"Hi, Jayden! Let me see you, my boy!" I crooned happily as I took the baby out of the arms of his mom, Haena, in front of the condo where I was visiting in California. He reached out to me easily and shifted his position to claim me as his own. Haena and her husband shook their heads in awe as they witnessed how comfortable Jayden was with me after only my second time meeting him since December of 2021.

"Hi, *Gomo*," Haena called me by the Korean word for *father's sister* as she hugged me tightly. Her husband joined us for a group hug.

Haena's husband helped me get my bags into my suite and took a moment to talk with me.

"You can't imagine how thrilled Haena is to have you in her life," he said. "She always wanted to be part of a loving family. Now that you've come into her life, she has that. She's felt a deep kinship with you, like she has finally found home."

Later, as we sat in the living room with Jayden contentedly playing with a toy in my arms, I was still blown away that we've found each other. Even as I relished this moment, I got choked up knowing how hard it must have been for Haena to be estranged from her family and living in a strange country without a family to call her own.

I'd been looking for her for years, but I'd been told that she lived in Oregon. My parents had even lied to me about where their granddaughter lived! I'd used every avenue available to track Haena down in Oregon, but I couldn't find her—because she never lived in Oregon.

While still trying to locate her, I took my pent-up frustration to start my mentor-mentee program in Long Island. Even in times of disappointment, God can still use us to do good works. Although helping the youth of Long Island gave me a focus, I still had a large hole in my heart.

My brother, Young Suk, called me in November of 2021, three days after they buried my father. He hadn't called to tell me about Dad's passing, but to ask me for documentation so that Mom could claim his assets.

"Dad didn't have a will, so Mom can't get her money," he continued. "Everything was in Dad's name, not hers. There's some paperwork I need you to fill out so Mom can access the bank accounts."

Ah, Young Suk, who had physically and sexually abused me for years, wanted a favor from me. Interesting.

"And I miss you," he told me on the call.

"You *miss* me?" I asked as an ironic, flat statement. "Do you mean you miss abusing me?"

"What do you mean 'abusing' you?" he asked, sounding shocked. "I don't know what you're talking about. I remember that one time I brought you some food that you really liked. That's about all I remember from us as children."

"Maybe I can remind you of what happened," I said, running through a short yet profoundly dark list of offenses that I suffered by his hand.

When I finished, he said nothing for a few moments. Then he tried to manipulate me with his response.

"Heawon, as a psychotherapist, you of all people should know that you need to let all of that go. Forgive me for your own sake."

How often throughout history has the abuser tried to demand that the victim offer blanket forgiveness for their transgressions? I wondered. *Well, not today,* I stilled my spirit. *I have no problem offering forgiveness when an offense is slight, accidental, or inconsequential. Young Suk's abuse of me had been profound, repeated, and traumatic.*

Unwilling to talk about the past any longer, I asked him about what paperwork I needed to secure. He didn't know.

I called the Korean consulate. Thanks to COVID, I waited on the phone for hours without success.

Then I had a thought. Young Suk told me that Haena was at my father's funeral.

"Young Suk," I said when I called him back. "I can't do this alone. I'll need Haena's help to reach the consulate."

"I can't give you her number without her consent," my brother said flatly.

"Then I can't help you get access to the money," I replied. "Put me in touch with Haena, and then I'll see what I can do about completing the paperwork you need."

After years of searching and asking, that's how I finally got Haena's contact information.

"Hello," a sweet voice on the other end of the phone had asked. "Is this Heawon? This is your niece, Haena."

I choked up as soon as I heard her voice. I told her that I'd been looking for her unsuccessfully for many years.

"I had no idea," Haena told me. "I never knew that you wanted to get to know me until my father called."

"I had been told you were in Oregon," I explained. "I used every avenue available to track you down, but I couldn't find you. I was beginning to lose hope…"

"No! I'm in Orange County in California," she told me. "That's why you couldn't find me!"

I didn't say much on the call, since my mother had told me that she'd trashed me to Haena. I couldn't blame my niece if she'd spent years thinking that I was the devil.

But I called Haena again a few days later.

"Can I come out to meet you?" I asked, not sure if Haena would like that idea.

"Of course you can!" Haena replied excitedly. "I want you to meet my husband and baby! Are you able to come in the week between Christmas and New Year's? I get a week off."

"Of course I can," I said excitedly. "But is it OK if just the two of us spend some time together for a bit when we first meet?"

On December 26, 2022, I flew from New York to California. Haena met me at the airport, and over dinner, I asked her questions about her life. At first, we checked each other out, not sure what to believe about the other because of all the lies we'd each been told. But we quickly learned that we were two peas in a pod. We shared similar values, and had both overcome many dark times in life to come out into the full sun.

Since that first visit, Haena and I have become like sisters. We share our life stories as well as our intimate thoughts and feelings, as if we'd known each other our entire lives. Neither Haena nor I had mothers who gave us the love and care we wanted. Knowing the kind of love I wanted from my own mother, I pour that depth of love into Haena and her family—to fill holes in both of our lives. Haena and her young family send that same love back to me.

Finally, the daughter of Korean Freud has a daughter of her own.

Acknowledgments

Writing a memoir was harder than I ever imagined, and surprises came which were more rewarding than I could have anticipated.

Margherita was the first woman in my life who showed me empathy without wavering. Her trust and belief in me as a valuable person and encouragement to own myself were instrumental to my personal growth. She was my best friend and surrogate mother.

Paduki and Cosmo, my golden retrievers, taught me what love and loyalty looked like. Their love was inexhaustible. They were the most potent medicine for my healing.

Special thanks to Edith Calhoun, professor of international studies at Adelphi University (1986–1988). She helped me find a place to stay when I first came to the US and then later helped me complete her course, even when I failed to show up for a test due to psychological distress. She also helped me get into an English as a second language (ESL) class and asked my classmates to share notes with me. Without her, I wouldn't have been able to complete my master's program.

Thank you to those at Eastern Long Island Hospital who generously supported me in gaining addiction counseling education, as well as those in acupuncture training at Lincoln Hospital.

Chris and Linda Haring, my neighbors who became my surrogate family, thank you for being there for me all these years, through good and bad. You have given me so much strength.

Although my search for you, Haena, brought ups and downs for more than a decade, my time spent looking was well worth it. Thank you for reading this manuscript from front to back and making suggestions; I know it was hard for you to read about your dad.

I'm forever indebted to Scott and Jocelyn Carbonara for their editorial help. They have been patient with my Konglish (Korean English)—correcting, replacing, rearranging, and fact-checking to make my story coherent and impactful.

Special thanks to Jenny Lisk, the ever-patient project manager, and Patrick Atkins, the greatest cover designer I could ever imagine.

Finally, thanks to everyone who has been a part of my getting here including: Jennifer Gimenez, Robin McKinnon, Marjorie Peter, Alison Poage, Karen McMahon, and Suzanne Link.

About the Author

Heawon Hake, LCSW-R, ASAC, has served as a director at Center for Marriage, Family, and Individual Counseling in Suffolk County, New York, since 2000. She provides direct care to clients while supervising other psychotherapists. She also makes time to conduct business coaching, and she sat on the board for the Eating Disorder Council of Long Island.

Heawon has expertise working with abused children and their families, providing residential and community-based therapies, and addressing substance misuse disorders. As a novice grant writer, she created an integrated community approach to working with individuals and families affected by substance abuse—a grant that yielded a quarter of a million dollars from New York State. Later, Heawon created and led a nonprofit organization that partnered young adults with mentors in Suffolk County, New York, to offer locals the high level of programs and services offered in New York City and Long Island.

Heawon graduated from Yonsei University in South Korea before moving to the United States in 1986 to start graduate school. After earning her master's in social work at Adelphi University, she trained at Gestalt Center of Long Island. Always learning, she later attended Pace School for Alcohol and Drug Counseling and studied acupuncture at Lincoln Hospital.

Heawon applies eclectic philosophies and practices in her work and personal life. When she's not serving members of her community or learning new therapeutic modalities, she spends time playing piano, ballroom dancing, gardening, cooking, running, meditating, binge-watching K-dramas, and smothering her furry kids with love.

Connect with Heawon at koreanamericanpsychotherapist.com or on social media @thewayofkap.

twitter.com/thewayofkap
instagram.com/thewayofkap

Made in United States
North Haven, CT
27 August 2023

40840451R00118